Scotland Journey

Scotland Journey

BARRY BLACKSTONE

RESOURCE *Publications* · Eugene, Oregon

SCOTLAND JOURNEY

Copyright © 2011 Barry Blackstone. All rights reserved. Except for brief quotations in critical publications or reviews, no part of this book may be reproduced in any manner without prior written permission from the publisher. Write: Permissions, Wipf and Stock Publishers, 199 W. 8th Ave., Suite 3, Eugene, OR 97401.

Resource Publications
An Imprint of Wipf and Stock Publishers
199 W. 8th Ave., Suite 3
Eugene, OR 97401
www.wipfandstock.com

ISBN 13: 978-1-61097-518-6

Manufactured in the U.S.A.

All Scripture quoted, unless otherwise indicated are taken from the Holy Bible, the Old King James Version!

*I dedicate this series of reflections to my dear wife, Coleen.
Thanks again for our first thirty years, and all the memories!*

Contents

Prelude: A Thirty-Year Dream *xi*
　　—*Proverbs 16:9*

1　An English Love Song　1
　　—*Proverbs 18:22*

2　Snow Squall on I-95　3
　　—*Job 38:22*

3　Herb-Crusted Salmon in Boston　5
　　—*Ruth 2:14*

4　Overnight Flight to Heathrow　7
　　—*Psalms 119:55*

5　Six Catholic Ladies from Massachusetts　9
　　—*Judges 5:29*

6　Christmas Tea at Harrods　12
　　—*Psalms 119:103*

7　Street Beggar at Euston Station　14
　　—*Luke 16:20*

8　Double-Decker Bus Ride through London　16
　　—*Psalms 48:8*

9　Backtracking to Buckingham Palace　18
　　—*Psalms 48:13*

10　Supper at Simpson's-in-the-Strand　20
　　—*Luke 14:16*

Contents

11 The Lion King at the Lyceum Theatre 22
    —*Job 4:11*

12 Extra Hour in England 25
    —*II Kings 20:10*

13 Willow Trees at Hampton Court 27
    —*John 14:2*

14 Yorkshire Pudding at Salisbury Cathedral 29
    —*Matthew 23:27*

15 Surprise at Stonehenge 31
    —*Joshua 4:6*

16 Balloons over Bath 33
    —*Daniel 8:2*

17 Cold Water at Cardiff 35
    —*Jeremiah 18:14*

18 Cruising through Cotswold Country 37
    —*Numbers 13:27*

19 Autumn on the Avon 39
    —*James 3:7*

20 Love Spoon in Llangollen 41
    —*Ephesians 5:254*

21 Barge Cruise to the Bryn Howel 43
    —*Job 38:25*

22 Worship Place at Wrexham 45
    —*John 4:22*

23 Chimes at Chester 47
    —*Psalms 89:15*

24 Light Rain in the Lake District 49
    —*Job 28:26*

Contents ix

25 Gifts at Grasmere 51
 —*Matthew 7:11*

26 Rendezvous in Scotland 53
 —*I Corinthians 13:12*

27 Entering Edinburgh 56
 —*I Thessalonians 1:9*

28 Feasting under the Firth of Forth Bridge 58
 —*Jeremiah 16:8*

29 A Cousin in the Country 60
 —*Luke 1:36*

30 Exploring Edinburgh 62
 —*Psalms 31:21*

31 A Man Called John 64
 —*John 1:6*

32 Edinburgh Castle 66
 —*I Chronicles 11:7*

33 A City on a Hill 68
 —*Psalms 121:1–2*

34 Holyroodhouse Palace 70
 —*Jeremiah 30:18*

35 Greyfriars Bobby 72
 —*Luke 16:21*

36 Shopping on Princes Street 74
 —*Matthew 7:7*

37 A Scottish Hot Dog under Scott's Monument 77
 —*I Timothy 4:4*

38 Britannia 79
 —*John 6:22*

39 Great Supper at the George 81
  —*Luke 14:16*

40 Jedburgh Jewelry 83
  —*Malachi 3:17*

41 Standing Stones on the Scottish Border 86
  —*Joshua 4:7*

42 Laughing All the Way to York 88
  —*Proverbs 15:15*

43 What's in a Word? 90
  —*Judges 12:6*

44 Strolling through the Shambles 92
  —*Psalms 48:12*

45 Rain in Rotherham 94
  —*Proverbs 16:15*

46 Window Shopping in Stamford 97
  —*Proverbs 24:32*

47 And I, Even I Only, Am Left 100
  —*I Kings 19:14*

48 Crossing the Cam in Cambridge 102
  —*Obadiah 14*

49 The Cambridge Seven 104
  —*Isaiah 6:8*

50 Last Night in London 106
  —*Nehemiah 8:18*

Postlude: Many Miracles 109
  —*Revelation 1:19*

Prelude: A Thirty-Year Dream

*"A man's heart deviseth his way:
but the Lord directeth his steps."—Proverbs 16:9*

MY DEAR wife and I got married in 1973, and within two weeks we had started a pioneer church in southern New Hampshire. Over the last 30 years, our life has been the Church of Christ. We have given ourselves to it 24–7. Our first five years in the ministry saw us working two jobs each, and when we finally started full-time in the pastorate, we still worked like we had two jobs. Coleen raised our two children while I rose up three more churches. Since 1980, I have been keeping track of the number of days per year we have directly or indirectly labored at 'church work.'

At the time of this writing, I have taken off just 32 days in which I haven't done anything connected to the Church I am now pastoring. I want this clear—these numbers don't mean I have worked 8-hour or 10-hour days all of these days, but it does mean that even on my so-called 'days off,' something has happened that has resulted in me doing something for the Lord and His people that day!

I have told many people that the best training I ever had for the pastorate wasn't my years in Bible School, but my years raised on a dairy farm in northern Maine. Dairy farming is a 365-day-a-year job, and the closest profession to it is the pastorate. In both occupations, the 'flock' and the 'folks' are always in need. We have forgotten today in the pastorate the basic concept of being a shepherd. A shepherd is on call 24–7, and he must be willing and ready to go and do, or he shouldn't be in the ministry to begin with (I Peter 5:2–4). Today, the average pastor has a 9-to-5 job with days off. I was not only raised on a dairy farm, but I also lived with an old-fashioned pastor who showed me by his example that I was a servant of the 'sheep' (Psalms 100:3). Today, it seems that in most situations, the 'sheep' are serving the shepherd. I didn't get into the ministry to be ministered unto, but to minister!

Some would ask how Coleen and I have done it, but I only reply that 'He has done it through us' (Philippians 1:6). We've had the privilege of pastoring four churches in 30 years and raising two children and a host of other people's children. It was to honor my wife and the sacrifices she has offered up through the years (Hebrews 13:15–17) that the Lord lay on my heart in 2003 to take her on a special trip to England, Scotland, and Wales. We chose those places because of a dream we had shortly after we were married. Because our honeymoon was cut short by our desire to get into the Lord's work, we started planning a number of times a get-away trip. We even went so far as a local travel agency to get fliers about possible trips to far-off and distant places. It was no very long before my heart's desire was to go back to the country of my origin. I have both English (Blackstone) and Scottish (Anderson) blood running through my veins. I also have a love of history and have read and studied much about that island in the North Sea.

Needless to say, our dreams were put on the back burner as we discovered just how much time and money it takes to pastor a church and raise a couple of kids. I must admit I hadn't thought of our dream for years until our youngest child graduated from Lancaster Bible College in 2002. It was then I discovered there was a little bit of money left over at the end of each month. Not telling my wife of my intent, I began to save and plan. It wasn't until I had the money in hand that I finally told Coleen of my desire to fulfill our 30-year dream. As I have done in so many aspects of my life, I couldn't take this trip without recording how the Good Lord works and cares for his children, even to the granting of a 30-year dream:

> *"Delight thyself also in the Lord; and he shall give thee the desire of thine heart!" (Psalms 37:4).*

Before you is a series of 'love stories;' to some, they might even be devotionals. I wrote them after I returned from this 30-year anniversary trip. As Coleen and I traveled across the Atlantic Ocean for 10 carefree and romantic days in England, Scotland, and Wales, I recorded certain observations and reflections from our journey. As with every aspect of my life, I can find God everywhere and hear His 'still, small voice' anywhere, even in a strange country among strange people. My prayer and aim for writing these memories and remembrances down is to challenge any that might read them to hang on to your God-given dreams; they too can come true. Joseph had dreams as a child (Genesis 37:5–10) that didn't come true until he was an adult (Genesis 42–46). Keep on dreaming, be patient, and see just how God works all these dreams out in your life! And maybe, just maybe, it is time for you and your wife to leave it all behind and venture off somewhere to rekindle the love of your past.

My life has been a "love story' in the making, whether my love for God, His people, our children, or the special lady the Good Lord gave to me in 1969. Scotland Journey is but one chapter in that "Love Story". Find a quiet place and join Coleen and me on this romantic trip to the fabled island in the North Atlantic.

—Barry Blackstone
October 23, 2003

1

An English Love Song

"Whoso findeth a wife findeth a good thing, and obtaineth favour of the Lord."
—Proverbs 18:22

For our 30th year wedding anniversary, I gave my wife an autumn trip to England, Scotland, and Wales. We had a wonderful time, just two strangers exploring the cities and towns and countryside of the United Kingdom. The trip was made extra-special by the simple pleasures we were able to enjoy and the God-given surprises along the way. Our tour was pretty much laid out in advance, but the best-laid plans always result in a detour or two. We even had in mind what we wanted to purchase beforehand, but even in that an unexpected find resulted in an unforeseen blessing.

My favorite English singing artist is Roger Whittaker. He has probably passed his most famous period, but to me his songs will always hold great memories. His songs like 'The Last Farewell,' 'Durham Town,' and 'New World in the Morning' still provoke wonderful remembrances of my past. So while looking for Scottish sweaters in Edinburgh, I found a CD by Roger Whittaker, and on it a song I had never heard before; entitled, 'All of My Life.' This song has become the theme song for my wife and me and the amazing 10 days we spent rediscovering our love for each other in the United Kingdom. Here are the words to this lovely love song:

> The stalk of grass tastes sweet upon my tongue,
> A tiny bird above begins to scold me.
> I stretch my toes up to the morning sun,
> And dream your arms of golden brown will always hold me.
>
> I shared my world with birds and beasts and space,
> I needed nothing else to satisfy me.
> But laying here I see your smiling face,
> I'm glad I didn't rest until you were beside me.
>
> Now I know why I walked that dusty road,
> I had to go back where I was to find you.
> Now I am not alone within my soul,
> You turned what was a house into a home.
>
> All of my life I will thank the Good Lord that I found you;
> All of my life with my love I am going to surround you;
> And taking the time to prove I love you, sure as you see the stars above you.
> All of my life, yes, all of my life, filling your life with love.

This English love song is a perfect melody of the love I have for the wife the Lord gave me. My prayer is that every time she hears it sung she will remember the magical days we spent on that island in the North Sea, and the second honeymoon we shared in our Scotland Journey!

2

Snow Squall on I-95

"Hast thou entered into the treasures of the snow?"
—Job 38:22

My wife and I left for our dream trip to England, Scotland, and Wales on October 23, 2003. We traveled with our daughter, Marnie, to the Concord Trailways Bus Terminal in Bangor, about 25 miles from our home in Ellsworth on the coast of Maine. We were going to pick up the 11:15 a.m. bus to Boston's Logan Airport, where we would take a plane to Heathrow Airport just outside of London. We left on a typical fall day in the middle of autumn; it was frosty, and a threat of snow was in the air.

As we boarded the bus in Bangor, Marnie took a picture of her adventurous parents and said goodbye. Then the bus driver announced the first movie, and I recalled a time over two years before when I had boarded the same bus, but my destination wasn't the United Kingdom but France. I was heading to Paris to pick up my daughter who had gotten sick on a short-term mission trip to Togo, West Africa (another adventure I recorded in a book called, "Rendezvous in Paris," published in 2010). The first movie they played that day was 'Rugrats in Paris;' this time the movie was, 'How to Lose a Guy in 10 Days.' My wife and I were going to be away for 10 days! (Our trip went fine and not once did my wife lose me, but interestingly, on the way back home, guess what was still playing on the Concord Trailways bus from Boston to Bangor: 'How to Lose a Guy in 10 Days!' The world tries, but a God-ordained love always prevails!

Our trip south to Boston by way of Portland was uneventful except for the weather just outside of Portland. As my wife watched the movie, definitely a 'chick flick,' I was reading an old book I had brought along for just such occasions. Suddenly, I looked up and saw we were driving through a snow squall that had completely blotted out everything around us. The flakes were huge and without number, except by God's tally. The roadway was still warm, so we were not delayed, as there was no accumulation, but the site was heavenly, if not glorious. There was no fear that the squall might delay our travel, so I sat back, watching and enjoying this 'treasure' falling on a fall day in late October.

Do you ever wonder why certain events happen when they do? Christians are not immune or exempt from snow squalls, delays, accidents, disappointments, or tragedies. Sometimes there is no certain answer or understanding of 'why?' When we finally get to the 'Answer Man,' we will understand better, but till then we need to look for the treasure in the storm. I have been making a list of items in my life I haven't understood to ask Him then. Don't take me wrong, I'm not complaining. I am simply underlining and highlighting the conundrums of my life—puzzles to be pieced together in another day and time. Until then, I am going to sit back and enjoy the ride, looking for the beauty that can be found in a snow squall on the interstate of my life. Believe it or not, I put this event down as the first of many miracles on our dream trip!

3

Herb-Crusted Salmon in Boston

"At meal time come thou hither, and eat..."
—*Ruth 2:14*

COLEEN AND I got to Logan Airport in Boston in the middle of the afternoon on our first day away from family and friends and 'flock.' The Concord Trailways bus driver dropped us off at the British Airways Terminal, and we immediately headed for the ticket counter. The lady was very helpful and nice, and I was surprised there were no lines (those would come later). The reason was simple: our plane wasn't scheduled to depart for nearly five hours!

With a slight English accent, the ticket agent processed our tickets and luggage and answered all of our questions (we had a few). My last question to her was where we might get a bite to eat. We hadn't eaten since breakfast, and all we got on the bus was water and pretzels. In our conversation together, I had casually mentioned that my wife and I were celebrating our 30th wedding anniversary on our trip. After the lady had finished putting us into the computer, she said she had to make a call. After a few minutes, she returned and informed us that we had been invited to eat at the British Airways Executive Lounge for supper in honor of our anniversary. Once again the Lord had within the first few hours of our trip prepared the way for a very special experience that will probably never be forgotten.

It took Coleen and me about 20 minutes to get through security. We then walked to the end of the departure gate area until we came to the end of a long hall. From there, we took the elevator down to the VIP lounge. Having never been in such an area, we didn't know what to do at first, but there was a receptionist who welcomed us and showed us to the dining lounge. Despite the fact we were traveling economy class (the old third class, back of the plane and all that); we were now being seated in the first class lounge at the British Airways Terminal in Boston.

Co and I picked out a table for two in the middle of the room, and then went to the table where all the food was placed. Coleen chose the eggplant-spinach parazonle for her main dish; I took a slab of their herb-crusted salmon. It was a meal fit for a king and queen. It was a special treat and totally unexpected—one of the best meals on the entire trip. As I sat in the executive lounge eating my warm salmon, I thought of the story of Ruth and Boaz's invitation for her to eat. Ruth didn't expect such treatment, yet that is just how the Lord often works. His Word is our daily meal, and just when we think we have tasted it all before, He gives us a special meal that is long remembered. It is far better to let Him plan our meals than to seek the same old, same old at the fast food courts of the world. Co and I left the Executive Lounge with full stomachs and rejoicing hearts for a special meal given to us by our Father and British Airways.

4

Overnight Flight to Heathrow

*"I have remembered thy name,
O Lord, in the night, and have kept thy law."*
—*Psalms 119:55*

THE FIRST call for Flight #0214 came around 7:55 p.m. For four hours, my wife and I had waited patiently for that call. We had filled those hours with supper, walking, reading, exchanging dollars and cents into pounds and pence (our first shock of the trip: I gave the lady $100 and she gave me 50 pounds and 50 pence!), and listening to fiddle music: a couple from Scotland with their two children was also waiting for the flight to Heathrow. While they waited, one of the lads played his violin. It was beautiful and just a prelude to our days in Scotland.

We boarded without any problems, and right on time the British Airways 777 took off. Within the hour, we were having another meal and settling in at 37,000 feet. It was Coleen's first overseas flight, and she was impressed with the meal but unimpressed with the temperature. The cabin in economy class was full and very warm; either other people were comfortable or the air conditioner wasn't working, but we couldn't convince the stewardess of just how hot we were. At 9:25 p.m., we flew over Eastport, an island off the down east coast of Maine where Coleen and I once lived. It was then a quick flight over Nova Scotia, and we were out over the vastness of the Atlantic Ocean. Somewhere around midnight I switched my wristwatch to London time (England is five hours ahead of east cost time) and tried to get some sleep. Sleep came hard because of the heat and excitement, so I did what I always do when I cannot sleep—I thought on the things of the Lord!

I have found that midnight is a great time to meditate on God. I live in a world that doesn't really know which god to believe in, but I like Paul "know whom I have believed" (II Timothy 1:12). Even those in Christian circles are tragically lacking in this area. Christianity is weak today in the unshakable certainty of just who Jesus is. I like what the disciples said when they were confronted with this debate: "And we believe and are sure that thou art that Christ, the Son of the Living God" (John 6:69). As I trusted the pilot for a safe overnight flight to Heathrow, I have put my trust in the Son of God that He will get me safely to His home in heaven. I am not trusting in the peace of the world, but in the peace that Jesus left (John 14:27). My wife and I were in perfect peace that night because we saw this flight as a God-ordained trip. We were safe in the belly of that 777 because we were safe in the hands of Jesus (John 10:28–29).

The false peace of the world can only dull your conscience and deaden your senses, but the "peace of God which passeth all understanding, shall keep your hearts and minds through Christ Jesus" (Philippians 4:7). That's peace—we might even call it 'perfect peace.'

5

Six Catholic Ladies from Massachusetts

*"Her wise ladies answered her,
yea, she returned answer to herself."*
—Judges 5:29

COLEEN AND I arrived at Heathrow Airport around 8 a.m. on the second morning of our dream trip to the British Isles. The ground was frosty, but the early morning sun was warming the air and melting the frozen dew. Once we were on the ground, our pilot announced that there would be a delay in getting to our gate. It seems it was an important day in England. The last three flights of the famous Concorde Supersonic Airplane were coming into Heathrow on the very day we had arrived for our first visit to the United Kingdom. As Coleen and I waited for nearly an hour to get to our gate, six Catholic ladies from Massachusetts were also waiting in the economy class cabin of our 777. We didn't know it at the time, but they would be traveling with us until we returned to this same airport nine days later.

Coleen and I disembarked and got our luggage. We passed through British Customs and got our passports stamped. By the time we found the main terminal, it was nearing 9:30 a.m. There waiting for us was our Cosmo tour guide. We couldn't miss her, for she was wearing what would become the familiar red uniform of the tour. She greeted us in a friendly British accent, but said we would have to wait a few minutes because there were six ladies not accounted for. Coleen and I found a cool spot near the door and waited. It wasn't long before our tour director came back with six middle-aged women in tow. You could tell at first glance they were all single, all very independent, and by their accent, all from the Boston area. As we boarded the shuttle bus for our motel in London, I said to Coleen, "This is going to be an interesting week with these ladies!"

A quick, snap judgment is always a dangerous thing, whether in sizing up people or making predeterminations about individuals. There are always two sides of the coin, and one should never judge someone until you spend a few days on a tour bus with them! Over the next week, Coleen and I got to know these six Catholic ladies from the Boston area. They were all friends who had traveled together on many a tour. Twice a year, they picked a place in the world to visit, and then simply go! They all worked for or had some connection to a telephone company in the Boston area. They loved the great cathedrals and churches we toured. We found them to be pleasant and fun, and before our time together was over, we had become friendly.

Coleen and I last saw these six ladies from Massachusetts as they picked up their luggage in Logan Airport at the end of our trip. We had shared an experience that took us back and forth across the Atlantic, besides traveling through the United Kingdom. First impressions are not always right! That includes your first impression of your future wife. I barely gave Coleen a look when she started attending my home church. She would say I had basketball blinders on. My senior year of high school was a year of sports without girls, but my dear Coleen was looking. Our eyes finally met 'across a crowded room' in the spring of 1969. For over 40 years now we have traveled together without a glimpse for another!

6

Christmas Tea at Harrods

*"How sweet are thy words unto my taste?
Yea, sweeter than honey to my mouth."*
—*Psalms 119:103*

COLEEN AND I arrived at the Euston Thistle Motel, just east of the famous Regent's Park, around 10:30 in the morning on October 24th. We found that our rooms were not ready, so we had time to plan our next day and a half in London. It was Friday, and we were not supposed to actually leave on our bus tour until early Sunday morning. As we talked to the tour director at the motel, we found that our time was really our own. The tour did have some activities planned, but we were free to do our own thing. Coleen and I decided to be adventurous and think outside the box!

Our first adventure was to hire one of London's famous black cabs and take a trip down to Harrods, one of the world's most well-known department stores. Coleen loves to shop, and she had her eye on some English tea. The ride took us about 20 minutes, and the cabbie was very friendly and informative. We traveled around Hyde Park until we arrived at Brompton Street. We got out about a hundred yards before the store and walked through the crowded sidewalks to the block that was Harrods. The building is five stories tall, and we learned, contains 330 separate departments. If you wanted it, and you can afford it, you could find it at Harrods.

We were surprised to find Harrods already decorated for Christmas, but as we walked from department to department, we realized we were hungry. It was nearly 1:30 in the afternoon, and we hadn't eaten since breakfast on the plane. Co and I found a café on the second floor and sat down to scones, croissants, tea with clotted cream, and jam. It was nice, if not expensive, and after lunch we continued our search for that special English tea.

It wasn't long before we discovered a tea department on the first floor. There my tea-loving wife went from tea to tea; trying to decide what tea she wanted to take home from Harrods. Finally, she came upon a 'Christmas Tea.' Each year my wife plans and shares a Christmas Tea with the ladies of our church. She decided that this year they would drink a tea she purchased in London. The attendant poured the Christmas Tea from a large container into a Harrods box. He put a 'Christmas Tea' label on it, and Coleen gave him a few pounds and some pence. If the tea tastes as good as it smells, it will be a great Christmas Tea 2003!

As we walked out of Harrods later that afternoon, I remembered the verse I have printed above. The new tastes and smells we experienced at Harrods are much like the experiences we can have with the Word of God and His Son, Jesus Christ. Walking through the Bible is like walking through the various departments of Harrods. There are so many tastes just waiting for us to experience, but in order to taste them, we must first be willing to take them into our hearts and minds!

7

Street Beggar at Euston Station

"And there was a certain beggar named..."
—Luke 16:20

INSTEAD OF taking a taxi back to our motel from Harrods, my wife and I decided to return by the 'underground'—the London subway system. Getting on the Piccadilly Line at Knightsbridge, we took a train to Green Park where we switched to the Victorian Line. From Green Park we traveled through Oxford Circus and Warren Street Station until we arrived at Euston Station, just a block from our motel. We were very proud of ourselves as we walked the final few yards to our home for the weekend; our first adventure into downtown London had come off without a bit of trouble.

Settling into our motel room, which was very elegant, by the way, we watched on British television the last Concorde to land in Heathrow. We unpacked and planned our only full day in London, deciding to buy a pass that would allow us to travel on the famous double-decker buses around London. This would allow us to stay in any one place for as long as we wanted. By the time we had finished our plans, it was supper time. The official meals of our trip wouldn't start until Sunday night, so once again we were on our own. After something as daring as we had pulled off in the afternoon, my wife and I were looking for something simple for supper. Believe it or not, we had noticed a Burger King at Euston Station when we passed through, so we decided to do something American while we were in England!

It was dark by the time we left the Thistle for Euston Station. The night air was cool, but not cold. It was fully fall in London, and with it came the changing of the trees. It was a pleasant walk down the block from our motel to the huge subway station at Euston Square. Out in front of the station was a large plaza where the city buses dropped off passengers for either the subway or the city train system, which also passed through Euston (actually pronounced 'Houston') Station. The sidewalks and streets leading up to the station were full of people coming and going.

As Coleen and I made the right-hand turn to enter the plaza, a young man in his 20's approached me with a magazine that looked like it had been read a hundred times. Unfamiliar with the ways of the street, I didn't realize at first that he was a beggar looking for a handout. As he approached and asked if I would be interested in buying his magazine, I first said, "No!" Then he asked if I had any change to spare. Without thinking, I reached into my pocket, pulled out a new 20-pound note, and handed it to him. Instantly, he began to run and shout up the sidewalk. He never said thank you, and it wasn't until I told my wife what I had done that she told me I had given the beggar nearly 40 dollars! The Good Lord must have thought he needed it, and sometimes your right hand shouldn't know what your left hand does.

8

Double-Decker Bus Ride through London

"As we have heard, so have we seen in the city..."
—Psalms 48:8

After nearly 35 hours with little sleep, my wife and I went to bed very early on our first night in the British Isles. Our dreams were of the day before us, a tour of England's fabled city: London on the Thames. We caught our first double-decker bus in front of Madame Tussaud's Wax Museum. Coleen and I had walked about half and hour from our motel to catch 'The Original Tour' bus. Our first planned stop was at Trafalgar Square. Being a history buff, I wanted to see the famous square up close and personal, and this is what we did. The traffic was busy, and the people were thick, but I had the time of my life walking the square under the shadow of the statue of England's most famous admiral: Lord Nelson.

Catching the next bus, we rode down to the House of Parliament, Big Ben, and Westminster Abbey. Coleen and I had our picture taken in Victoria Tower Gardens beside the Thames River. It was a beautiful day in the city with a light breeze and the temperature in the upper 50's. People thought it was cool, but it was the perfect autumn day for

Coleen and me. The trees were changing, the people were friendly, and we were having the time of our lives.

After walking up to Westminster Abbey, we boarded the bus for our first trip across the Thames by way of Lambeth Bridge. From there we walked down to the Imperial War Museum, my Harrods of the trip. Returning to the Thames, Co and I had 'fish and chips' at a small café right on the banks of the Thames. We watched the boats go by right across from Westminster Hall and its famous clock tower.

After lunch we boarded our double-decker bus again and didn't stop until we got to St. Paul's Cathedral, where we had our first disappointment. The Cathedral was under repair, and it cost a small fortune to get a look inside. It was in London we discovered that most of England's great cathedrals are not churches any longer, but museums! From there we were off to London Bridge (the New London Bridge, for the old London Bridge of 'London Bridge is falling down' is now located in Arizona!). We walked across London Bridge and decided to walk all the way to Tower Bridge and then walk across it. From there we were off to Buckingham Palace.

The sights were wonderful, the weather was beautiful, and the experiences were marvelous. I can't remember the last time I had more fun in a city, and our day in London reminds me of another day coming when I will explore a fabled city by a river (Revelation 22:1): the New Jerusalem (Revelation 21:10–27). As with London, there will be great sites to see; but unlike London, there will be no cathedral, no abbey there (Revelation 21:22). There will be no admission fees to the wonderful mansions, and we won't have to travel about on a double-decker bus, despite how thrilling it was for my bride and me.

9

Backtracking to Buckingham Palace

*"Consider her palaces, that ye may tell it
to the generation following."*
—Psalms 48:13

On our list of sites to see in England were Buckingham Palace, and the colorful ceremony of the changing of the guard in front of the Queen's residence in London. After our walk across Tower Bridge, Coleen and I boarded our double-decker transport for a drive along the Thames River. We crossed and re-crossed this famous waterway a couple of times as we made our way toward Buckingham Palace, located just beyond Westminster Abbey. The weather was still warm and the sites breathtaking as we wound our way through the busy traffic of this massive city. Caught up in the sites, we missed our first opportunity to get off in front of the Palace, and by the time we realized our mistake, we were a 10-minute walk away. Instead of pressing on, Coleen and I decided to backtrack to Buckingham Palace.

On the way to the famous house, Coleen discovered a simple tea shop. A year before, a young lady from our church had visited London and brought Coleen back some special tea. Coleen had already looked for it at a number of shops, but it was during our stroll back to Buckingham that we found it. For her, the walk had already been rewarding! For me, it was the splendor of seeing this magnificent mansion from afar and walking right up to its front gates. In front of the palace is the spectacular bronze and marble Victoria Monument, erected in 1911 and constructed using more than 2,300 tons of marble. A marble Queen Victoria looked down upon me from the east side of this massive monument, and an exuberant bronze winged Victory angel peered down from the top of it.

Beyond this large open area, and behind a barricade of railings and gates, stood Buckingham Palace. It was impressive; even though we found out we had arrived too late for the changing of the guard. We learned that we were in the season when the guard only changed in ceremony on alternating days, and even on those days, it takes place at 11:30 a.m. Coleen and I had only gotten to the palace by 1:30 p.m. I spent my time taking pictures and enjoying the small crowds looking the palace over. Co and I got our picture taken in front of the main gate, and that picture is now sitting on my desk as one of the great images of our second honeymoon. We also discovered that at this time of the year (late autumn), the guards change from their well-known red uniforms to green uniforms. Through the iron bars, we were able to see two of these royal guards standing beside their famous boxes!

We didn't get to go into the main grounds, but just being outside was enough to say we had been to one of the planet's most renowned mansions, a story we will tell for many years to come, until we arrive at our own mansion (John 14:2), a palace that will put Buckingham to shame.

10

Supper at Simpson's-in-the-Strand

"A certain man made a great supper..."
—Luke 14:16

RETURNING EARLY from our tour of London, Coleen and I made preparations for an evening out. We had been able to get tickets for supper and a show at one of London's finest eating places: The Savoy—Simpson's-in-the-Strand; and one of London's greatest theatres: The Lyceum, where the award-winning musical, "The Lion King," was showing. Around 5:00, a bus arrived to pick up Coleen and me at the Thistle Motel. We were actually joining a group that was finishing their British tour. As we drove downtown, we were told this about Simpson's-in-the-Strand:

Founded in 1828, Simpson's was originally a cigar divan where gentlemen came to drink coffee, play chess, and read the journals of the day. It was so popular that it became known as the 'home of chess.' Over the years, many famous tournaments have been played there, including the 1993 Kasparov-Short World Championship match. In 1848, John Simpson introduced the renowned Bill of Fare, and Simpson's established itself as the classic British eating house. Gladstone and Disraeli, prominent English prime ministers, were regular patrons. Robert Scott ate his last meal there before departing for the Antarctic and his legendary death.

Dropped off in front of Simpson's, we were escorted upstairs and ushered into the most elegant restaurant my wife and I had ever seen. The waiters and waitresses were dressed in formal attire. We too were dressed to kill. As we looked over the menu, we decided for starters on the home-cured bresaola with shaved pecorino, cold-pressed extra virgin olive oil, and cracked black pepper. Our dinner guests had terrine of red snapper and roasted vegetables with roasted sweet red pimento dressing. For our main course, I had chosen poached Scottish salmon served with homemade mayonnaise, new potatoes, and a mixed leaf salad. My wife had roast breast of turkey filled with cranberries, onion, and sage carved from the trolley and served with bubble and squeak, fine French beans, and tomato shreds. Our eating companions had char-grilled swordfish steal with a warm Nicoise salad. Then for dessert Coleen and I had one of the richest puddings we had ever tasted: dark chocolate parfait with white chocolate shavings and a rich chocolate sauce. Our new-found friends had tropical fruit delice served with pressed red berry coulls.

These fine foods were all served by a team of waiters and cooks who brought the main courses out on trolleys. Little did Coleen and I imagine that before our trip was finished, that we would eat in a more refined restaurant than Simpson's-in-the-Strand? The food was excellent, the service professional, and the atmosphere elegant. I picture my first meal in glory to be even more heavenly than my supper at the Savoy (Revelation 22:2). A romantic supper at a fancy eatery is of course just the appetizer to a great show to meet the King!

11

The Lion King at the Lyceum Theatre

*"The old lion perisheth for lack of prey,
and the stout lion's whelps are scattered abroad."*
—Job 4:11

IT WAS a short five-minute walk from Simpson's-in-the-Strand to the Lyceum Theatre where Disney's "The Lion King" was playing. The Lyceum is considered the premier venue for theatre in London's West End. Coleen and I arrived to discover that we not only had floor seats, but we were only six rows back from the stage and orchestra pit.

At 7:30 p.m., the play opened with the full cast singing "The Circle of Life" around Pride Rock. If you can imagine human beings turned into animals, then you can imagine what Coleen and I saw as lions, zebras, elephants, and a myriad of other animals walked down the aisle beside us and came out from behind the screens before us. Julie Taymor was the costume designer, and she did an amazing job. Each of the main characters, from Rafiki to Zazu to Mustafa, was wonderful as they and the supporting cast sang and danced across the stage. Because both Coleen and I had seen the movie, we had some idea of what was coming, but the wonder of seeing it in a live production was simply wonderful!

I enjoyed the songs as much as the costumes, from young Simba singing "I Just Can't Wait to Be King" to Pumbaa belting out "Hakuna Matata." The orchestra, conducted by Clement Ishmael, and the other singers, Rob Edwards as Scar and Nataylia Roni as Nala, brought a new meaning to a live production. I have only seen a few professional plays in my time, but "The Lion King" at the Lyceum is the finest yet. For two hours, my wife and I held hands and watched with open hearts, minds, and mouths as the drama played out before us. As the scenes changed, from Pride Rock to Scar's cave to Rafiki's tree, the drama built. We were then off to the elephant graveyard, the gorge, and the desert beyond. In two hours, we were transported to a place where good does overcome evil, and the lion does get the lioness in the end. From Prideland to Shadowland and back, we traveled with these colorful characters. When it was over, all we could do was stand and cheer such a truly marvelous performance.

As we left the theatre for our motel in Euston, it began to sprinkle. The rain couldn't dampen our spirits as we both knew we had shared something special in the theatre district of London. Tim Rice, the lyricist, perhaps said it best in the signature song of "The Lion King:" can you feel the love tonight? I could! Sometimes it isn't enough to tell somebody that you love them—you need to show them. The evening Coleen and I spent in the west end of London Town was the most expensive evening I have ever experienced, yet I would do it again because there are some experiences that only money can buy! If I never do it again, I can say that I have taken my dear wife to a fancy restaurant and to a Broadway play, and that it was beyond all expectations! I realized that night that in just two days, I had fallen in love with my precious wife again. If you talked to her today, she would say the very same thing. It was as if we had backtracked 30 years and were once again on our first date together!

12

Extra Hour in England

*"And Hezekiah answered, It is a light thing for the shadow
to go down ten degrees: nay, but let the shadow
return backwards ten degrees."*
—*II Kings 20:10*

WHEN COLEEN and I planned our special trip to the British Isles, we did not do it because of the changing of the clock. We didn't know until we returned from our special evening on the town that we would be getting a bonus hour on our only full day in London. Like in the United States, England also turns its clocks back an hour in the autumn season. We actually got 25 hours to explore London Town on our only full Saturday in the United Kingdom.

The next morning, we were heading out on our bus tour of England, Scotland, and Wales, but on October 25th, we had an extra hour to spend in London. We had seen much and traveled many a mile to take in the most illustrious places of the fabled capital. We had even gone to a couple of places that were not in our original plans—perhaps the most special of all. When each adventure ended, and we were off to new sights and sounds, both my wife and I could feel that our Good Lord was leading all the way. And then to top if off, He planned it so we had an extra hour to remember and rejoice over the special experiences we had shared together. Our extra hour was shared at the Thistle Motel, celebrating our marvelous day together in England's storied capital!

Amidst all the scientific and technological triumphs we witnessed in London, I believe it was the simple extension of time that gave me the greatest thrill that day. It was not part of the tour; it was not part of the price; it was not part of the plan; yet it became a part of that day, that 25-hour day in London. There is joy and happiness that comes when the Lord surprises you with a bonus. For Coleen and me it was the bonus of an extra hour added to the most special night of our entire trip. Only the Lord has such timing, such control of time. Only He can look down through a year and add 60 minutes, 360 seconds to an already wonderful day. If the backwards turning of the clock hadn't happened that evening in London, it still would have been an amazing Saturday, and Coleen and I would have still praised the Lord for working out all the details connected with the Simpson's restaurant and the Lyceum Theatre. But as with Hezekiah when he found out he was getting extra time, it is an unexpected gift and a wonderful enjoyment.

Coleen and I went to sleep that night dreaming of what we had seen and heard and experienced, but we also were dreaming of what lay ahead. Our trip had only begun and we could only imagine what our Tour Director had in store for us over the next week. If a single day in London had produced such memories, what would a whole week include? Were there still some extra joys yet to be revealed? There were!

13

Willow Trees at Hampton Court

*"In my Father's house are many rooms; if it were not so,
I would have told you that I go to prepare a place for you."*
—John 14:2 (RSV)

Our United Kingdom tour began early on the morning of October 26th as I got up at 6:30 a.m. to get our bags out for the porter. By 7:30 a.m. we'd had breakfast and were meeting our tour group in the lobby of the Euston Thistle. Here we also met our Cosmo guide, Roseann Forster, and our Cosmo bus driver, Eon Walker. When all the heads were counted, there were a total of 28. The group broke down like this: the six interesting ladies from Boston, one couple from Michigan, one couple from Tennessee, four people from Indonesia, five people from Australia, four people from Thailand, three people from the Philippines now living in the U.S., and a couple from Maine on their second honeymoon. We left the hotel a little after eight for our first stop at Hampton Court Palace.

Once again the Lord had given us wonderful weather as we drove up to the Tudor Palace of King Henry VIII. The morning had started out frosty, but by the time we started our tour of the grounds of this immense house the sun was out and it was warming up. Because we were at the end of the tourist season, all we had time for was a quick walk through part of the 60 acres of stunning, riverside gardens, and an outside view of the massive mansion of 1,000 rooms (yes, you read that correctly!). The luxurious retreat had been a favorite of many of Britain's kings, queens, and a favorite of mine Oliver Cromwell. As Roseann put it, "Henry the Eighth was so inspired by it that he spent three of his honeymoons there!" Coleen and I were happy just to spend a part of our second at this palace.

As we walked around, I marveled at the impressive architecture. We peaked in the windows to see the opulent interiors and colorful paintings on the walls. Coleen loved the flower gardens, which despite the lateness of the season, were still colorful. I also loved the many swans and ducks and Canadian geese about. The trees were trimmed and groomed in wonderful patterns, and you could see that it was a palace prepared for a king. The gardens ran all the way down to the Thames River, and along part of the banks was a group of willow trees. Our new friends from Australia took a picture of Coleen and me standing in front of that part of the garden; it was a place right out of heaven for me!

We only had about an hour to walk and stare, so there was little time to explore William III's Privy Garden, known as the Maze, and according to Roseann, 'a sure place to get lost!' We took pictures and smelt the roses and enjoyed the warm autumn air around Hampton Court. As we left for the bus, I thought of the verse I have printed above. Heaven is going to be a wonderful place if it is anything like the gardens and mansion of Hampton Palace. I hope mine is on the banks of a river with plenty of willow trees around!

14

Yorkshire Pudding at Salisbury Cathedral

"Woe unto you, scribes and Pharisees, hypocrites! For ye are like whited sepulchers, which indeed appear beautiful outward, but are within full of dead men's bones, and of all uncleanness."
—Matthew 23:27

GETTING BACK on the bus, Roseann told us that we were heading for Salisbury and its famous celebrated cathedral with one of the world's highest spires—an impressive 404 feet! The trip should have only taken us about an hour, but we were delayed by an accident on the M3 motorway, much like our super highways. A horse trailer had turned over blocking our way, but after reading a few pages of an old book I had brought along for such delays, we were quickly on our way again. Soon we turned off the motorway to worm our way through a back lane into Salisbury. On the way, we passed through the towns of Upper Wallop, Lower Wallop, Middle Wallop, and Never Wallop. I am not kidding. It had started to cloud over, but still no rain. Just after noon we got our first view of Salisbury Cathedral's Spire as it reached for the heavens, dominating the city skyline.

We were given two hours to explore the cathedral and eat lunch. The ancient church was really a graveyard in a church. Like with St. Paul's in London, Salisbury Cathedral was just a museum. The rock work was amazing, its height was dizzying, but the interior was filled with 'dead men's bones.' For the first time, I understood what the Lord meant when he preached to the scribes and Pharisees. There were sepulchers for the rich and famous under the floor of the massive church, and in the walls as well. Wherever you walked, you were walking on the dead. Coleen thought it was eerie, but I thought it was sad that people believe you could come closer to God by being buried in a church. As we worked our way around the different chambers, we eventually arrived at the café; yes, a café. We had lunch in the restaurant in back of the basilica.

Coleen and I both had the roast beef, carrots, and potatoes, and for dessert we tried the Yorkshire pudding. The lunch cost us $30.65, but the memories of Salisbury will forever be of the spiritual deadness we felt. Leaving the 'city of the soaring spire,' we were filled with sadness that a once religious country could turn their houses of worship into tourist traps, and their chapels in cafes. The monument that soared above the city and pointed to Heaven had very little to do with heaven, or the one they said was worshipped there. The pudding was good, but the parish was poor. Just to keep the place up they had to ask for donations from the tourists. The flock of Salisbury had an amazing fold, but it was just a cemetery of former churchgoers. All I could think as we boarded the bus for Stonehenge was that if America doesn't repent, it too would soon be turning its churches into cafes and cemeteries!

15

Surprise at Stonehenge

"What mean ye by these stones?"
—Joshua 4:6

ON THE first day of our travels through the British Isles, the summary of our tour read like this:

"Meet your tour director and traveling companions and depart at 8 a.m. for a memorable day's sightseeing: the ornamental gardens of Hampton Court, Henry VIII's magnificent Tudor palace; Salisbury, the 'City of the Soaring Spire;' before passing Stonehenge, one of England's most intriguing mysteries. Stop in the elegant Georgian city of Bath, famous for its Roman relics; then across the Severn Bridge, a tribute to modern engineering, into Wales and Cardiff!"

I had read this description over and over in the weeks leading up to our 30th anniversary trip, and one phrase kept jumping out at me: 'before passing Stonehenge?' Did that mean we were only going to see the famous standing stones from a distance, a quick look out our bus window? One of the reasons I wanted to go to England was to see the world's most recognizable group of rocks. Just to pass by without a stop or a chance to get a picture beside the stones seemed disappointing at best. However, shortly after we left Salisbury, Roseann brought up the language of the tour booklet, asking, "Can you just pass Stonehenge?" It was then the Good Lord worked another miracle: we would not be passing Stonehenge, we would be stopping there!

Like with most of England's well-known sites, Stonehenge has become a tourist magnet. It was very crowded when we drove up to the parking lot across the road from the Stonehenge site. There was a fence keeping out all but those who would spend five pounds to walk close to the standing stones (you can no longer walk up and touch them). To witness this amazing series of stones on the Salisbury plain was worth fighting the crowds for a good shot. A man from our tour took our picture with the stones behind us. We were there, even if the $64,000 question wasn't answered: how and why here?

Historians believe the stones were placed on this small knoll in Wiltshire between 1800–1400 B.C. Some think it was a place of worship, while others believe it was used to chart the movement of the moon and sun. The rocks are not of the same type as are normally found on the plain, and how those primitive people managed to move these massive stones over large distances is still a mystery known only by the ancient people that moved them. As we drove off to our next stop in Bath, Roseann gave her opinion above the carved stone monument. She gave the scientific and cultural answer, but in my opinion she didn't give the Biblical answer. About the same time the people of England were laying their standing stones, Joshua was laying God's standing stones in a plain next to the Jordan River in Gilgal!

16

Balloons over Bath

"I saw . . . and I was by the river of . . ."
—Daniel 8:2

It took us a little over an hour to travel from Stonehenge to the beautiful city of Bath-on-the-Avon. On the way, we passed through a military area where we experienced our first 'tank crossing' sign! We arrived in front of the Abbey of Bath around three o'clock. We had until dark to explore this amazing city built on a hill by a river.

As Coleen and I started our walking tour, a group of hot air balloons came floating over the city. The sun was just beginning to lower in the western sky, and the reflection of the balloons against the granite hillside was spectacular. The sunlight was also reflecting off the copper-colored buildings, turning them golden. The trees along the Avon River were also picking up the final rays of our fourth day, and they too had turned yellow. I was able to get some wonderful panoramic shots of the Beechen Cliffs and the outstanding Georgian architecture seen in the elegant crescents and terraces of the structures built there.

As Coleen looked for a place for us to exchange some dollars into pounds, I took a quick walk back to the Avon, where I was able to get some beautiful foliage photographs with the barges tied up along the river bank. While I was snapping pictures, Coleen discovered that the best place in town to exchange money was Christopher and Banks, England's version of a Wal-Mart. Walking by the famous Roman baths, Britain's only hot springs and at one time the greatest Roman religious spa in Northern Europe, we finally found the department store on Henry Street. This time we got 114 pounds and 50 pence for $200!

After we got a bit of English money in our pockets, we went in search of a few Christmas presents. We decided that gifts from Britain would be unique Christmas presents for 2003. As we traveled from store to store, we were also on the lookout for postcards. Coleen had decided that she was going to scrapbook our trip, so postcards would make a colorful addition to the scrapbook pages. On the way, we crossed Trim Bridge, and then worked our way back to a small park by the Avon called Parade Gardens. This was my favorite part of the city. The sun was almost gone by this time, but the view up to Pulteney Bridge was awe-inspiring to me. It was starting to cool down as the sun finally set behind the cliffs, and the balloons had also floated out of sight, but hand in hand, Coleen and I wandered about without a care or concern. I felt that I had finally arrived at the kind of place I was looking to experience in England. The streets were not crowded, and the atmosphere was charming and delightful. We didn't find any presents, so we saved our pounds and pence for another day. Just taking in the sights along the Avon River was worth the trip. I hated to return to the bus, and I will never forget the balloons over Bath and the hand-in-hand evening I spent with my wife on the banks of the Avon.

17

Cold Water at Cardiff

*". . . or shall the cold flowing waters
that come from another place be forgotten?"*
—*Jeremiah 18:14*

It was nearly 5:30 in the afternoon by the time we crossed the famous Severn River Bridge into Wales, heading toward Cardiff, the capital of this fabled country. It was the only place on the tour where we had to pay a toll. By the time we arrived at the Cardiff Moat House at Circle Way East, Llanedeyrn, South Glamorgan, it was dark.

We were greeted by the motel manager, who gave us a little taste of the Welsh language. Russel Ham said this to us: "Croeso I Gymru, ag I Gwesty Moat House Caerdydd!" (Which means, "Welcome to Wales and the Cardiff Moat House! We do hope you enjoy your stay at the hotel.") Checking into our room, we discovered twin beds (was this any way to celebrate our second honeymoon?), but we learned that this was very typical of motels in the United Kingdom. After we unpacked, we had supper at the Moat Motel Restaurant. I tried their mutton, and I was no impressed! It was here we got to know the three young people, Oscar, Eric, and Leah from the Philippines, who all worked in the United States. They were on a 'friend's holiday.' It seems that on occasion they pick a place to go and get together to travel; two work on the east coast and one on the west coast. They were pleasant, and Coleen and I enjoyed getting to know them over our week together. They spoke wonderful English and were funny and easy to be around.

We had a restful night's sleep despite the twin beds, but woke early because our bags had to be out by 6:15 a.m. It was then we discovered that we would be taking cold showers before our new day of exploring the Cotswold. Needless to say, we were not impressed with the Welsh ways: twin beds, mutton, and cold showers, but it was here we also experienced our first full-English breakfast, including Cumberland sausage, back smoked bacon, grilled tomatoes, rosti potatoes, baked beans, scrambled eggs, all kinds of juices, tea or coffee, Danish pastries, various fruit, and kippers. It was enough food to keep the average person going for a week!

By 7:30 a.m., we were back on the bus and heading back toward England. On the way, we passed the Millennium Stadium, the 'temple of world rugby,' their national sport. We didn't have time to see Cardiff Castle, except from afar, or Cathays Park, for our tour was heading to the Wye Valley and the romantic ruins of a 12th century abbey. It was foggy in the valley as we wound our way through the foothills of southern Wales. It was a cool, crisp day, but the hopes for a sunny day were not far off, for our ultimate destination was Gloucestershire, England. Both Coleen and I were happy to see Wales pass behind us; but maybe our second night in the fairyland of Wales would be different? And it was!

18

Cruising through Cotswold Country

"And they told him, and said, We came unto the land whither thou sentest us, and surely it floweth with milk and honey."
—Numbers 13:27

COLEEN AND I enjoyed the first day of our bus tour through the British Isles, but we really enjoyed our second day as we traveled through Gloucestershire and the beautiful Cotswold Hills.

Our first stop that morning was at Tintern Abbey, one of the oldest abbey ruins in the land. Located on the banks of the Wye River, this ancient pile of rocks is impressive despite being nothing but ruins. We stopped long enough to get a few pictures and enjoy the peacefulness of the river valley before moving on. It was here I discovered from Eon, our driver, that the Wye is a salmon river. The season for fishing was passed, but just getting my picture taken on its shores was enough for me. Eon also told me that a weekend for four on a salmon river might cost as much as $52,000! (The sport of kings!?!)

We wound our way through the Wye Valley as we followed the flow of the river, crossing and re-crossing its course a few times. Eventually, we drove into the plains leading up to the Cotswold Hills. We were once again back in southern England, in an area known as the English Midlands. Our first stop in this picturesque place was the picture-book town of Broadway. As we rode along, Roseann kept us entertained with stories of the region and trivia like how the monks of Tintern Abbey made their mortar. Ready for this? They created it out of grass, mud, pigs' blood, sand, lime, and water!

Broadway was Coleen's and my favorite small town of the tour. I got this off a postcard we picked up in Broadway:

"The delightful unspoiled village of Broadway is considered by many to be the finest Cotswold village in Hereford and Worcester. Its long, broad main street and its greens are lined with lovely old cottages and fine Cotswold houses, nearly all constructed from golden Cotswold stone!"

As Co and I walked the streets, the sun came out. I stopped at a small Methodist church for a peak, and Coleen found the parsonage (manse) with two bottles of milk and a paper at the door. I took a picture of her and them together. Co also found her favorite store in the UK, the Edinburgh Woolen Mill; here she made her first major purchases of the trip: a wool scarf and fleece jacket.

Coleen and I really hated to leave Broadway. It was a peaceful and tranquil place with few people. It truly was a land that 'flowed with milk and honey,' and we truly enjoyed the taste and flavor of the Cotswold Hills!

19

Autumn on the Avon

*"For every kind of... bird... is tamed,
and hath been tamed of mankind."*
—James 3:7

OUR NEXT stop in Hereford and Worcester was the famous Stratford-upon-Avon, the birthplace of England's best known writer, William Shakespeare. Just outside of town we stopped for a group picture at Ann Hathaway's—Shakespeare's wife's—illustrious cottage, a beautiful thatched-roof home. It made for a nice photograph and a wonderful keepsake of our trip and the group we toured with. We then moved off to Stratford itself and a ride by Shakespeare's homestead. The old house was in pretty good shape, for how old it was. Not being Shakespeare fans, Coleen and I moved on to other things, like celebrating autumn on the Avon with a romantic picnic lunch.

Before Roseann cut us free, she took us to the famed statue of 'The Jester' of Stratford-upon-Avon: "The fool doth think he is wise, but the wise man knows himself to be a fool; o noble fool! O worthy fool!" From this starting point we were free to wander through the shops of Stratford and get a bite to eat.

Co and I did a bit of Christmas shopping before buying a sandwich and heading down to the Canal Basin for lunch on the Avon. We picked a bench right on the bank of the river where the birds were gathering and the canal barges were cruising. It was a lovely autumn day with the temperature near 60. The sun was warm and the atmosphere stunning. We had a wonderful view down the Avon River with the high spire of Holy Trinity Church in the background. The trees along the river were all a golden color, and just behind us was the Gower Memorial, one of the many landmarks of Stratford-upon-Avon. It was then my attention was drawn to the numerous birds feeding and sunning themselves on the banks of the river. For as many birds on the shore there were twice as many birds in the river, and every one of them seemed to be looking for a handout from the tourists and locals enjoying autumn on the Avon.

There is something about fowl in the fall, in my opinion. I was taken by the large swans and huge numbers of Canadian geese. We had seen quite a few at Hampton Court, but there must have been a geese convention going on at Stratford! I was especially drawn to a goose with a crippled leg. My wife was also drawn to this weaker member of the bird community of Stratford. Coleen had picked up a package of granola at the breakfast table that morning and decided to feed the goose instead of eating it herself. I fed it the rest of my sandwich as well. I know the Lord said that "your heavenly Father feedeth them" (Matthew 6:26), but on that early afternoon in autumn, my wife and I decided to help Him out, at least with one Canadian goose struggling to make ends meet on the banks of the Avon River in Stratford!

20

Love Spoon at Llangollen

"Husbands, love your wives..."
—*Ephesians 5:25*

We left Stratford-upon-Avon around 1:00 p.m. on October 27th, heading back into Wales for our second night on the road. However, before we traveled on to Wrexham, we made a stop in Llangollen, one of the most memorable stops on the whole trip.

Llangollen in Conwy is located on the Dee River. How I enjoyed the rivers of our tour, and one of the prettiest was the Dee. Most of the rivers we crossed or walked beside were narrow but full. When we arrived at Llangollen, the Dee was shallow and cascading over layered, granite ledges. I was able to talk to my first fisherman who was actually fishing: a brown trout fisherman not having much success. One of the highlights of Llangollen, for there were many, was the discovery of an ancient local custom known as 'lovespoons.' Seeing as Coleen and I were on a second honeymoon, we couldn't pass this tradition by. This is what we learned about the history of 'lovespoons':

"The ancient custom of giving 'lovespoons' originated in Wales, and reached the height of its popularity in the 17th century. Men would spend many hours hand-carving lovespoons with elaborate symbols to present to their sweethearts as a token of their affection on such special occasions as courtship, engagements, weddings, anniversaries, birthdays, and christenings, and as a sign of their serious intentions. Lovespoons were also given as a gift of love, warmth, and friendship to friends and members of the family. Many of the symbols carved would be handed down for generations. Some of the symbols and their meanings were as follows: heart—affection and love; hearts entwined—hope of love returned; links—loyalty and faithfulness; trapped ball—the heart trapped in the cage of love; key hole—the door to the heart and home; lock—safety and security; soul signs—heartfelt affection; flowers—passion and fertility; horseshoes—good luck; diamond—good fortune; anchor—desire for home and its comforts; ship—a smooth voyage through life; wheel—commitment to the relationship; cross—good faith and the sanctity of marriage; harp—the music of love; bells—harmony, unity, and marriage; and rope—for the entwining of souls."

For our 30th wedding anniversary spoon, I bought one that contains a carving of hearts (for affection and love), hearts entwined (hope of love returned), and a star in the middle (for eternity!). There are many ways to tell a wife how much you love them, but in a distant corner of the British Isles, you can do it through a carved, wooden spoon!

21

Barge Cruise to the Bryn Howel

"Who hath divided a watercourse for the flowing waters..."
—Job 38:25

THE SECOND memorable event at Llangollen, Wales, was a 90-minute ride on a motor narrowboat on the Llangollen Canal between Llangollen Wharf and the Bryn Howel Motel. Built over 100 years ago by Thomas Telford, the Llangollen Canal is 46 miles long and drops only one inch per mile in elevation. The crowning jewel of the canal is the Pontcysyllte Aqueduct, England's tallest navigable aqueduct, towering 126 feet above the River Dee. The canal flows quietly through the beautiful Vale of Llangollen, and its system of locks and docks is a testimony to the amazing engineering ability of a hundred years ago. Our guide told us that the Telford Canal was connected to the nation-wide system of canals, and that it was possible to take a boat all the way back to London, well over 200 miles away!

Our tour group got on Peter and Pip's narrowboat at the Llangollen Wharf around 4:00. Before we finished our ride it would be dark, but the sites we saw in the fading light of an autumn day were beyond description. Here are my highlights: sitting on the bow of the boat as Peter guided the 30-foot barge through the narrow canal leading up to the aqueduct; crossing the aqueduct at four miles per hour while looking down on the River Dee and the fall foliage; helping Peter maneuver the narrowboat around the lock on the other side of the aqueduct (I didn't do much!); heading up a side canal toward the Bryn Howel and being the only boat on that section of the canal; watching the sun set behind the Welch hills to our west while cruising by a flock of sheep; having a Coke and talking with Pip about why they started taking tourists like us on the canal; taking a group picture as we huddled together in the two person-wide narrowboat; buying a small, hand-painted change purse painted by Pip herself for Coleen; helping Peter dock the boat at the wharf in front of the Bryn Howel; and helping our guide Roseann and Coleen off the narrowboat.

Our afternoon in Llangollen ended at the motel known as the Bryn Howel, where we waited for Eon to pick us up with the bus. The Bryn Howel was built in the 19th century as a country home by a local businessman by the name of Bryn Howel. The inside was beautiful with oak paneling, ornate plaster work, and unique fireplaces. Co wanted me to dance in front of the fireplace, but I can't dance! It was a very romantic end to a very romantic kind of day. The slow, quiet ride through an amazing engineering accomplishment was only added to by the mystic and mysterious motel on a mountain overlooking Llangollen. You can get to the Bryn Howel by car or bus, but if you're ever in Llangollen, Wales, I recommend taking a narrowboat to its doors!

22

Worship Place at Wrexham

"Ye worship ye know not what..."
—John 4:22

AFTER A nearly 12-hour day, our tour bus finally stopped for the night in the northern Welch town of Wrexham (pronounced with a silent 'w'). Its draw to fame: located within city limits was one of the seven wonders of Wales! We saw the church lit up as we entered Wrexham, but it was not until after supper that Coleen and I decided to take a walk around town and see this massive structure up close and personal. I found this history in a pamphlet I picked up on sacred places in Wales:

"The stupendous Tudor tower (or steeples) of St. Giles Wrexham is justly numbered among the 'Seven Wonders of Wales.' Statue-bedecked, richly decorated and lavishly pinnacled, it stands 147 feet high, proudly distinctive among the tall modern buildings of 'the metropolis of the Borderland' and clearly visible for miles around. It also has a twin across the Atlantic, a replica built in the 1920s at Yale in the USA to honor that famous university's benefactor, Elihu Yale of Wrexham. This 'great Welsh American'—'born in American, in Europe bred, in Africa traveled, and in Asia wed'—lies buried only a few feet from St. Giles' tower. But there is also much more to see within this almost cathedral-sized, cathedral-atmosphere 'city church,' set in a quiet oasis near the center of busy modern Wrexham. Begun in about 1330, but lavishly remodeled in the late 15th century and magnificently extended in the early Tudor period, many centuries of development and use have each left their mark on it. Variety indeed is the keynote of St. Giles. Thus, for example, the sturdy pillars and arches of the nave are 14th century, as are the big carved stone corbels between them, which once supported the lower roof. In the later 15th century, the church was heightened with an upper 'clear story' of light-giving windows, the present 'angel roof,' and a huge east window. Notable features of this light-filled channel include repositioned 14th century 'sedilia' or 'priests seats,' carved with an array of 'green men' peering from oak-boughs; and the exceptionally fine wrought-iron screen across the entrance, probably given by Elihu Yale and dating from 1707. Above the chancel arch—to continue the catalogue of features from many periods—are the substantial remains of an early Tudor wall-painting of 'The Last Judgment,' rediscovered under whitewash in 1867. Flanked by the kneeling Virgin Mary and John the Baptist, the Christ sits enthroned on a rainbow above souls issuing naked or shrouded from their graves . . ."

I will not mention again another church or cathedral in England with such detail, but I am afraid in this island land they worship their churches more than the Christ!

23

Chimes at Chester

"Blessed is the people that know the joyful sound..."
—Psalms 89:15

October 28th, our sixth day in England, began early, much like all the days before: up by 6:30 a.m., luggage out by 7:00, breakfast by 7:30, on the bus and off by 8:00, and hearing Roseann's favorite phrase, "Golly gum drops, aren't we in for a nice day!"

Within an hour of leaving The Wynnstay Arms Hotel in Wrexham, Wales, we were pulling into the walled city of Chester, England. Like Bath before it, Chester had been a principle Roman town in its day, and many of the old Roman gardens could still be seen. Once Roseann gave us the layout of the city and when we needed to be back on the bus, Coleen and I were free to do our own exploring. Two goals kept us focused: exchanging some dollars into pounds and buying more film for the cameras.

The Lord had given us another beautiful day as the sun began to take effect on the frosty start. Our first stop was outside Chester Cathedral and the chimes tower. We arrived just in time to hear the chimes strike on the half-hour—they were heavenly! They weren't the Westminster

Chimes—my favorite—but the Chester Chimes were just as charming. Coleen and I took a walk on the old Roman wall walkway behind the cathedral and got to hear the chimes a number of times while in the city; the fall foliage, ancient chapel, and chimes placed our walk around Chester as one of the best mornings we had on the tour.

We also took a walk down Bridge Street, where the Dee River also passes through Chester, and past the well-known black and white half-timbered buildings and two tiered arcades called 'the Rows.' This series of underground shops contained just about anything you would like to buy, and at the end of the street was a bank where we got 109 pounds and 50 pence for $200 US. It was also here that we got up close and personal with the Eastgate Clock, built to honor Queen Victoria's 50th anniversary. The town presented the clock to her (she loves clocks), but then they kept it!

With our hour almost up, Coleen and I spent our last few minutes in Chester looking for film and walking back to the bus. On the way, we passed the Dee River Bridge and heard the chimes strike on the hour. The hour of departure had come, and as we came around the last corner, sure enough our bus was waiting to transport us to our next destination. I know that when the Lord comes for His Church, He will use a trumpet (I Thessalonians 4:16) to call His children, but if it is as sweet a sound as the chimes of Chester, then I can understand why even the 'dead in Christ' will be stirred from their graves and why we that are 'alive and remain' (I Thessalonians 4:17) will also be caught away. Even in the bustle of a busy city, the Chester chimes could be heard.

24

Light Rain in the Lake District

"When he made a decree for the rain..."
—Job 28:26

WHEN WE left for our tour of the United Kingdom, everybody told us to take an umbrella because it was sure to rain. Except for a few sprinkles in London on the second evening, Coleen and I hadn't experienced a rainy day. Even on the day of our trip to Scotland, it started out sunny and warm. The sun was still shining when we left Chester for Edinburgh, but the further north we traveled, the cloudier it became, and as we passed Liverpool, Manchester, and Lancaster, a light rain began to fall. We had entered the national park called the Lake District. As a postcard said, "The majority of English lakes are found here, and the Lake District comprises parts of Cumberland, Westmorland, and Lancashire. The area is rich in mountain massifs, noble valleys, dark woods, and gem-like stretches of water."

It is also very remote and contained many wonderful sights, even through a light rain! For the next two and a half hours, we wound our way through moor and vale; through small villages and tiny hamlets; around large lakes like Windermere and small lakes like Grasmere. The road was narrow and the traffic was slow, but the sights were spectacular with the low-hanging clouds touching the tops of the hills. The side hills were a dull red and the trees a dull yellow. An evergreen could be seen on occasion, but with the low light of the cloud-shrouded sun, everything was dull—but it was the most beautiful dull I have ever witnessed! Added to the foliage were the endless rock walls that divided the fields and meadows we passed. In each pasture was a flock of sheep. It was here we saw all the different colored sheep of England. There were white ones and black ones, black-faced ones and brown ones. It was here my wife got the idea that she wanted a Scottish sweater with all the colors of the sheep of the United Kingdom in it (she did find one in Edinburgh!).

I believe our trip through the Lake District of western England was one of the nicest rainy forenoons I have ever spent. Each corner brought a new sight, a new color combination, a new image of England. From rock barns to delightful manor homes to the smallest house in England (In the town of Windermere, we passed a tiny two-story home actually built over a small creek. The story was told that the house was built to take advantage of a loophole in the local tax law), Coleen and I marveled in the country setting of the Lake District. Despite the rain, it was an interesting and meaningful journey.

I have discovered over the years that some of the best blessings in my life have come in the rain. When the Lord decrees rain, we still should look around and seek a sight or sound or smell that is made more meaningful because it has been seasoned by rain. If on that day, you are traveling with the love of your life, then any rainy day is a good day.

25

Gifts at Grasmere

"If ye then, being evil, know how to give good gifts unto your children, how much more shall your Father which is in heaven give good gifts to them that ask him?"
—*Matthew 7:11*

OUR ONE and only stop in the Lake District of England, and our last stop before we crossed over into Scotland, was at Grasmere, the home of poet William Wordsworth. This is what I found written on a postcard about Grasmere, Cumbria: "This small village is found in a beautiful setting on the main road from Ambleside to Keswick and is known by many who are attracted to Grasmere by the fame of William Wordsworth. The small lake beside the town is part of Lord Lonsdale's commons and is leased to the National Trust which has created a footpath along the west shore. The island in the lake, however, is privately owned. William Wordsworth and his wife, Mary, are buried in the churchyard of the Parish Church of Saint Oswald in Grasmere Village."

Needless to say, Grasmere was another favorite small-town experience for us. While my wife looked for Christmas presents, I took pictures of the fog-covered hills and fall-covered moors. The rain was still falling as we made our way into town, but not enough for an umbrella.

We had driven into Grasmere shortly before one in the afternoon. We stopped to get a bite to eat, and Coleen and I had a wonderful lunch in a small sandwich shop just inside the town limits. The sandwich was good, and the sweets for dessert were grand. Looking at our watches, we realized we had a few minutes left over for some shopping. We were still on the lookout for special Christmas presents, in particular for our son, Scott. Scott is a golfer, and we were hoping we might get close to the world-famous golf course of St. Andrews. As it worked out, beside the sandwich shop was a small store with plenty of gifts from the area. Sure enough, in the hat section was a golf cap with the symbol and name of St. Andrews on the front. We knew that this would be a special gift for our son, and when we got back on the bus and discovered we would not be going anywhere near the golf course, we were happy we had found the hat.

For six days, my wife and I had been looking for something special for our son, and when we finally found it we were excited and pleased. If we know how to 'give a good gift' to our son, how much more does our heavenly Father know how to please us? When I first set my sights on taking my wife to England, I felt that the Father was behind it. The more I look back on this trip, the more I believe it was a 'good gift' from God to Coleen and me. In 30 years, I hadn't been able to save much money, and yet this year, I could! Picking up a gift for our son in Grasmere was nothing compared to the gift of Grasmere from God to us!

26

Rendezvous in Scotland

". . . Then shall I know even as I am known."
—*I Corinthians 13:12*

AT 2:46 p.m. on October 28, 2003, Coleen and I and the rest of our British Isles tour group crossed the border into Scotland. I felt like I had come home. One of the reasons my wife and I made this journey was Scotland. My mother's mother's mother was an Anderson. As a child, I remember visiting great-grandmother Anderson in Canada. She was very old when I was very young, but from those early years I became fascinated with Scotland. If there was one country of the world I had always wished to visit, it was Scotland, and now I was within its borders.

From Grasmere we had followed the M6 to the Scottish border. Traveling through Cumbria, the last English county before Scotland, we began to see less countryside and more fog. The flocks of sheep increased as we neared the border, as did the anticipation in my heart. It was as if I was homesick for a land I had never seen, yet it seemed so familiar. Except for the sheep, it was as if I was returning to my home county in northern Maine. I knew that I would soon find out why I had such a strong desire to see the land of my forefathers. Every passing moment, the excitement built as we came closer and closer to the border of this fabled land. And then we were there! Our first stop in the Scottish Lowlands was in Gretna Green, Dumfries and Gallaway, Scotland! What a thrill!

I knew I had arrived in the land of my great-grandmother when in the very first store we walked into was the Anderson 'tartan.' There from wall to wall were all the different tartans of all the different families of Scotland in alphabetical order, and guess who was first: Anderson! The Anderson colors are a soft blue and gray, and the Anderson crest could be bought on everything from cups to golf balls. It was not hard to decide what I would get my mother for Christmas. It was as if I had made a rendezvous with my past and all those from my Scottish family. It felt like home, and I felt at home. The Anderson name was everywhere, and little did I know just how connected I would be before we left the land of the Andersons.

As we quickly got back on the bus for Edinburgh, I thought I ought to feel the same way about another land and family. Paul wrote of a 'homesickness for heaven' (Philippians 1:22–24), and Jesus preached of living every moment in the mystery of our next life and homeland. How can we take so lightly the prospect of Heaven when we live daily on the verge of eternity? I marvel how I live sometimes as if I will live here forever. Every day and every hour we ought to live in the excitement, loaded with expectancy, ready to cross over. I experienced that on the border of Scotland, and I will experience it again, for I am living now on what Edgar Page called 'Heaven's borderland.' In his classic church hymn, he writes this:

"I've reached the land of corn and wine, and all its riches freely mine; here shines undimmed one blissful day, for all my night has passed away. My Savior comes and walks with me, and sweet communion here have we; He gently leads me by the hand, for this is Heaven's borderland. A sweet perfume upon the breeze is borne from ever vernal trees, and flowers, that never fading grow, where streams of life forever flow. The zephyrs seem to float to me, sweet sounds of Heaven's melody, as angels with the white-robed throng join in the sweet redemption song. O Beulah land, sweet Beulah land, as on thy highest mount I stand, I look away across the sea, where mansions are prepared for me, and view the shining glory shore, my Heaven, my home forever more!"

Crossing over into Heaven will be for me like our crossing over into Scotland, our journey ended!

27

Entering Edinburgh

". . . what manner of entering in we had . . ."
—I Thessalonians 1:9

OUR JOURNEY through the Scottish Lowlands from Gretna Green to Edinburgh took us nearly two hours: from late afternoon light to total darkness. On the way, we did pass the infamous town of Lockerbie, Scotland, site of the 1988 terrorist plane crash. I thought, as we passed the sleepy little town in an unknown region of southern Scotland, just how small our world had gotten since terrorism had started its terrible rampage. When Roseann reminded me of the date, I thought to myself that it couldn't have been that long ago, for it was as fresh in my mind as 9–11. Yet it had been 15 years since Lockerbie was put on the world map. Solomon spoke in Ecclesiastes of 'a time,' and we are living in 'a time of anger!'

By the time we arrived on top of the hills overlooking Edinburgh, the light rain of the Lake District was falling again. The huge city was lit up, and the Firth of Forth (the bay) could be seen behind the city lights. It took us a while to work our way through the busy traffic of Edinburgh to the Greens Hotel at 24 Eglinton Crescent, an 18th century gothic-style house—actually, four houses joined to make the motel. Coleen and I soon discovered that this would be the most elegant hotel on our tour.

Getting in out of the rain, we walked into a small, old-fashioned, Victorian lobby; Coleen was impressed from the start, despite the fact our room was on the third floor. The beautiful staircases and banister leading to our floor were something out of an old Scottish novel (Coleen's favorite reading material). Climbing each set of stairs brought us to a wonderfully-decorated landing. It was a tiring climb after nearly half a day on the bus, but each floor brought its own 'oohs' and 'ahs' from my dear wife. By the time we arrived at our room in the back of the third floor, she was already in paradise. Opening the door to our room only brought more adjectives from her mouth. The room was huge, and despite the twin beds, more like a suite. We had never before stayed in a hotel with such large rooms. It had a sitting area and plenty of room to spread out, and the next day we would discover it also had a 'million-dollar view' of Edinburgh!

The hotel had a marvelous restaurant on the first floor, where we would eat a number of meals, but perhaps the most unique aspect of the old hotel was the elevator. After walking three flights of stairs, we decided to find an easier way to our room. Just down the hall and around a couple of corners was an old-fashioned elevator. I had only seen them in movies—you know the ones where you have to close two gates, no automatic door there. The interior was also open so you could see the elevator shaft. Coleen and I felt as if we had been transported back to the 19th century and into one of those romantic books my wife loves to read. Coleen would say to this day that the moment she entered the Greens Motel we started writing our own romantic novel!

28

Feasting under the Firth of Forth Bridge

*"Go into the house of feasting,
to sit with them to eat and drink."*
—*Jeremiah 16:8*

OUR FIRST great treat in Edinburgh took place within the hour of our arrival at the Greens Hotel. Unknown to us, Roseann had made reservations for supper at an old-fashioned Scottish pub called the Two Bridges—so called because it sat between the famous Firth of Forth Railroad Bridge and the Firth of Forth Road Bridge. I had seen on TV pictures of the Firth of Forth Railroad Bridge, one of the most recognizable structures in the world. It is noted as being one of the earliest iron railroad bridges constructed, and at the time of its construction, the largest. As we drove from our hotel over to North Queensferry, Roseann told us this about the bridge: The piers of the bridge run 80 feet below the waterline, and the towers of the bridge rise 360 feet above the waterline. The bridge is a cantilever in design and runs 3,300 feet from side to side of the Firth of Forth. The small town we were going to was also a favorite vacation stop for Robert Louis Stevenson of *Treasure Island* fame.

Feasting under the Firth of Forth Bridge 59

When we drove up to Two Bridges, Eon parked the bus just across the street, right under the Firth of Forth Bridge. The bridge was all lit up, and the rain had stopped. Once again I had to look twice to see if I was really where I was. After dreaming and reading about such places, it is hard to imagine when you finally get to them that you are actually there. It was too dark to take pictures, so a postcard would have to do, but little did Coleen and I know that the best part of the evening was yet in front of us!

Roseann had made arrangements so Coleen and I could have a table by ourselves, still on our second honeymoon. We were seated at a window table looking out toward the bridge. Despite the fact the pub was decorated for Halloween, it was a very romantic place; candles on the tables, lights down low. The supper was wonderful, and just as we were finishing our dessert, in walks a man with his bagpipe. Our trip description had told of an evening with Highland dancers, bagpipers, and the infamous ceremony of the Haggis. Because of the lateness of the season, that part of the tour wasn't available, but Roseann knew a bagpiper by the name of Neel Innis, so she invited him to come to the Two Bridges and play for us!

Neel played a series of old Scottish tunes and then a medley of national songs, with a few American tunes and an Australian song for our Aussie friends. When he started playing "Amazing Grace," Coleen began to cry and I cried inside. It was a beautiful evening that we wished would never end. We did get our picture taken with Mr. Innis and bought one of his CDs to remember him by. What a special treat we had under the shadow of the Firth of Forth Bridge–the end of the first chapter of our romantic novel set in the backdrop of Scotland!

29

A Cousin in the Country

"And, behold, thy cousin..."
—Luke 1:36

I FOUND it hard to get to sleep after our evening at Queensferry, Scotland. It was well after midnight before I stopped writing down thoughts for future 'Scotland stories.' Little did I realize that one of the best was going to happen early the next morning?

When I opened the blinds to our third-story, ceiling-to-floor windows, I couldn't believe the view the good Lord had given us. Climbing the three-story staircase was now well worth the effort. Because the Greens Hotel was taller than any other structure in the area, Coleen and I had a panoramic view of the Old Edinburgh skyline. The sun was shining and we knew we had a very special day in front of us.

Our first stop was in the Greens restaurant for our first Scottish breakfast. The food table was well-stocked, and at first I thought that was all it was going to be until the waitress began bringing out more plates full of food. The Victorian style restaurant and the English china our food was served on only added to the already Scottish atmosphere. By 8:45 a.m., we were full and ready for our day-long tour of the

Scottish capital. It was then that Roseann informed us that she wouldn't be leading our tour for this day. It seems that the Scots don't like the English leading tours through their city, so Cosmo had to hire another tour guide to do Edinburgh, also known as the 'prince of cities, part of the tour. By this time, we had gotten used to Roseann and liked her style, so most of us were disappointed at first, but only until our 'big Scot' arrived.

Roseann introduced him as Sky Stuart, but his appearance made me think there was something familiar about him. He was decked out in full Scottish attire, and his kilt looked light blue and gray. Only the good Lord could have worked out such a detail, but as Stuart spoke he made mention that his last name was Stuart, but on this day he was actually wearing the tartan of his mother's mother: an Anderson. I couldn't help myself—before he stopped talking I raised my hand and introduced myself to a distant cousin. In all our travels and through all the towns we had explored, with all the people we had met and all the guides in Edinburgh, it was an Anderson that was sent to our tour. The special blessings from the Lord were adding up on this anniversary trip. Under the shadow of Edinburgh Castle, Coleen took a picture of me and my cousin—it doesn't get much better than that.

We might be left widowers. We might be strangers and pilgrims on this earth, but no matter what happens, we can never be called an orphan. We have a Father in God and a Brother in Christ, and no matter how far we roam, we have cousins in every corner of the world. If God could bring Sky and me together, you need to be looking for a Christian cousin or two in your little corner of the world. No matter how far we roam, we have family around us!

30

Exploring Edinburgh

*"Blessed be the Lord: for he hath shown me
his marvelous kindness in a strong city."*
—Psalms 31:21

OUR TOUR of Edinburgh began with an explanation by our Scottish Guide, Sky Stuart, of the two Edinburgh's:

"Old Edinburgh is the southern part of the city, encompassed by the castle and the Royal Mile; beyond them are the areas of Southside, the Grassmarket, and Canongate. To the south of the Royal Mile, you will find the Royal Museum of Scotland and the Festival Theatre, a venue presenting fine drama and opera. Edinburgh Castle and the Royal Mile are Old Edinburgh's main attractions (we would see both!). We are going to spend out morning exploring this part of the city, which will give you a potent sense of history embodied by the splendid clutter of old sandstone buildings. We will give you time to walk through Holyrood Park and get a glimpse of Holyroodhouse, the queen's residence when she is in Edinburgh. North of Waverly Bridge is Edinburgh's new town, where Old Edinburgh expanded during the 18th century as part of a typically-Georgian example in town planning. Above Princes Street is George Street, with handsome Charlotte Square and St. Andrew Square at either end. You will get a chance to explore this section of the city this afternoon. The elegance and unity of Georgian architecture—an exhilarating contrast to the equally-splendid Royal Mile—can be appreciated as such locations as Queen Street Gardens, the Royal Circus (a circular residential street), Great King Street and Drummond Place—all north of George Street—as well as around Morsay place, west of Queen Street Gardens.

Edinburgh is Scotland in microcosm. In this vibrant capital city, buildings do not overpower the spectacular landscape of hills and crags that march across the southeastern horizon. Yet Edinburgh's buildings—from the old houses of the Royal Mile (including John Knox's house) to the elegant Georgian terraces and crescents of the new town—are outstanding complements to the city's natural setting. Few capitals seem to reflect the history and culture of their country so potently. Edinburgh's famous castle sits on a craggy promontory, Castle Rock, made inaccessible on three sides by steep cliffs and with a long descending ridge on the fourth side. The city's layout is linear, a pattern set by Castle Rock and Castle Ridge, of which the Royal Mile descends to the Palace of Holyroodhouse. This is our first destination. Let's go exploring!"

With that opening introduction, Eon started the bus and we were off to discover the mysteries of Edinburgh. I wondered if that is how John felt after the Lord gave him a sketch of the New Jerusalem (Revelation 21–22). Could he not wait to visit the city himself? I can't wait!

31

A Man Called John

*"There was a man sent from God, whose name was John."—
John 1:6*

For me, one of the first memorable sites on the Royal Mile we passed was the home of John Knox, one of my favorite Scottish heroes. In my own research, this is what I found . . .

"Little is known about this famous Scottish reformer's early life, except that he was born John Knox in Scotland sometime between 1505 and 1513. We don't even know the date or place of his birth. Somewhere between 1530 and 1540, Knox was ordained a Roman Catholic priest, but by 1542 he was preaching against the Church. The change came somewhere between 1540 and 1546, when John Knox met George Wishart and was converted. Knox also followed the reform teaching of another great Scottish reformer, Hamilton. Hamilton had been martyred for his faith (Revelation 2:10) in 1528 and by 1546, Knox's mentor, Wishart, was burned at the stake. Shortly after this event, John Knox was arrested and served his sentence as a galley slave for 19 months in France.

Knox returned to England in 1549 but was forced to leave the country for Germany when the reign of Bloody Mary began. Living in Frankfort, Germany, where he was a pastor to a small group of English refugees, Knox came under the influence of John Calvin. After moving to Geneva, Knox spent a few years under the Presbyterian and Calvinistic tutelage of Calvin before preaching in Dieppe, France, and then returning to his homeland. In 1555, Knox married Marjorie Bowes, to whom he had been engaged for a few years, and they produced two sons. During this time, Knox also wrote two important works: *Predestination* and *First Blast of the Trumpet Against the Monstrous Regiment of Women*. Eventually, Knox took up the reform cause in Scotland and began preaching against the evil of the papal church. Arrested by Queen Mary Stuart in 1560, Knox was tried but miraculously acquitted (II Timothy 4:17).

John Knox spent the remaining years of his life preaching and lecturing in Edinburgh and St. Andrews, fighting Queen Mary of Scotland and Bloody Mary of England. His 'hell-fire and damnation' messages stirred the two monarchs, but during Knox's trips away from Scotland, the reform party had grown strong and powerful. All the monarchs could do was tolerate the man, of which it was said, "Here is one who never feared the face of man."

One of the greatest contributions of Knox to the Reformation was his *Book of Discipline*. In it, the great reformer set forth the basic principles for the guidance of the new Reform Church. The book underlined the importance of education in the New Church and urged the State to start educating every child, a radical concept in the 16th century. As with his birth and early life, so with his death: little is known except that he died in Edinburgh in 1572.

32

Edinburgh Castle

"And David dwelt in the castle..."
—*I Chronicles 11:7*

DURING OUR walk through Edinburgh Castle, I kept a timeline (in military time) of the things we saw. Here are the highlights as I wrote them down right after Coleen and I returned to the United States:

0930—Began our tour of Edinburgh Castle. When we entered the main gate, there were statues of Robert the Bruce and William Wallace, two more of my favorite Scottish heroes.

0950—Reached the top of the castle, and what a view! It was a perfect day weather-wise. The sun was out and warming up after a frosty start.

0955—Co and I went through the Great Hall, saw Wallace's huge sword (or so they say), a glorious hammered-beam roof, and an amazing array of weapons!

1005—Walked through the 'vaults' that contain the crowned jewels of Scotland. Also saw Jacob's Rock, which claimed to be the very stone that Jacob used as a pillow! It is on this stone that the kings of Scotland were crowned, beginning with King David. (Like Israel, Scotland's first crowned king was also called

David.) It is called the 'Stone of Scone' or destiny! The collection is called 'the honors of the kingdom'

1015—Walked by the One O'clock Gun, a 25-pounder that blasts off a single blank charge from the Half Moon battery at 1 p.m., except on Sunday. It was not Sunday, but we are too early to check our watches.

1017—Co took a picture of me beside a huge 1449 cannon, Mons Meg, that could shoot a huge stone ball two miles.

1030—Took pictures of the Firth of Forth. Sky said the mouth of the North Sea was 25 miles down the 'firth' (bay).

1035—Co loved Margaret's Chapel (12th century), the oldest standing building on the hill. It was made by the first king of Scotland (King David) upon the death of his mother. This is also the oldest building in Edinburgh itself.

1050—Took panoramic photos of Salisbury Crags, a rugged hill to the east of the castle.

1057—Read an excerpt from the Declaration of Arbroath from a postcard I picked up in one of the castle's gift shops. The Declaration was signed in 1320 and shows just how much the Scottish people desired and still desire their independence: "For, as long as but a hundred of us remain alive, never will we on any condition be brought under English rule. It is in truth not for glory, nor riches, nor honour that we are fighting, but for freedom, for that alone, which no honest man gives up but with life itself."

1105—Left the castle for a trip down the Royal Mile, the distance between Edinburgh Castle and Holyroodhouse.

33

A City on a Hill

"I will lift up mine eyes unto the hills, from whence cometh my help. My help cometh from the Lord..."
—Psalms 121:1–2

Before we left Edinburgh Castle for a ride down the Royal Mile to Holyroodhouse, I walked to the edge of the southern cliff and took one final look at Edinburgh in context of its majestic fortress on a hill. The famous landmark dominates the capital city's skyline just as the castle has dominated Scotland's long and colorful history. This is what I had learned in our two-hour tour:

"Perched on an extinct volcano, this fortress is a powerful national symbol to the people of Scotland. The castle's story is the story of Scotland. The stronghold of Eldyn was first recorded before 600 AD, and by the Middle Ages, it had become a mighty fortification and the royal residence of Scotland's kings and queens. Since the Bronze Age, it has witnessed much of the nation's rich past, including the birth of Mary Queen of Scots' only child, James VI, who united the crowns of Scotland and England, as well as Cromwell's Roundheads and the Jacobite Risings. A rich mix of architectural styles reflects the castle's complex history and role

A City on a Hill 69

as both a stronghold and the seat of kings. Crown Square, the principle courtyard, was developed in the 15th century and, in contrast, the Scottish National War Memorial was added after the First World War in 1918. Besides the Square and War Memorial, the castle contains the Great Hall, built by James IV, the Moon Battery created in the late 16th century, and the 'Stone of Destiny,' taken to Westminster Abbey in London in 1296 and not returned until 1996. The castle contains some of the oldest surviving regalia in Europe!"

I was impressed with the layout of the castle and all the cannons and massive walls, but in conclusion, the best part of the fortress was the view it offered of Old Edinburgh, the Royal Mile, and the hills surrounding the city. Despite the size of the city and its castle, the area is dominated by the dramatic Salisbury Crags and by Arthur's Seat, a high, round hill. Like Jerusalem before it, the people who built Edinburgh Castle and the surrounding town found strength in the hills. Hills not only afford protection from enemies and weather, they also produce a particular kind of strength. The ancient Psalmist said it best when he wrote, "I will lift up my eyes unto the hills, from whence cometh my help."

As I stood on the castle mount and took a 360-degree look, the power of the view was overwhelming to me. I could see why the citizens of Edinburgh were so proud of their city, and why Edinburgh Castle is the best-known and most-visited of all the famous sites in Scotland!

34

Holyroodhouse Palace

". . . and the palace shall remain after the manner thereof."
—Jeremiah 30:18

The short ride from Edinburgh Castle to Holyroodhouse along the Royal Mile was filled with splendid buildings and wonderful history as Sky Stuart explained where we were going. We stopped in Holyrood Park just beside the famous residence. It was a minute walk to one of the side gates of the Queen's Scottish palace, where we heard this:

"Ancient Holyroodhouse was part of the Abbey of Holyrood, but was built in its present form as a royal palace for King Charles II. The severe non-classicism of the courtyard block reflects the distinctly English fashion of the time; nevertheless, it exudes Scottish history. The State Apartments of Charles' palace is luxurious and grand, crammed with artifacts and paintings elegantly displayed beneath superb stucco ceilings. Deep in the historical apartments is the bedchamber of Mary, Queen of Scots, and the adjoining closet where, in 1566, her secretary and confidante, David Rizzio, was stabbed to death by associates of the Queen's delinquent husband, Lord Darnley."

Because of the time factor, we were only able to walk around the outside of the palace, but even that was impressive. Coleen had become a fan of Mary, Queen of Scots, on this tour, and anything she heard about this very tragic lady sparked an interest. We walked to a point where we could see one of the oldest parts of the palace, James V's Tower. It was here that Mary was held captive for her final years of life. On the back side, we could still see the ruins of the abbey on which the massive structure was added. In a back corner, we found a private garden, and despite the lateness of the season, there was still some beautiful color in the flowers and plants. I took a picture of my wife next to the lovely site, 'a rose among roses.'

Our final few minutes at Holyroodhouse were spent just gazing through the huge iron bars that separated us 'common folk' from the 'royal folk.' One of the thoughts that struck me there was how so-called 'royal people' keep themselves in fancy prisons. Holyroodhouse was nothing but a prison. Instead of keeping people in, as most prisons do, these fancy palace prisons were created to keep people out. The more of the history I heard of Holyroodhouse, the more I knew why royal people need more closets to hide their terrible deeds and secrets! As I walked away from the impressive palace, I was glad I had only come for a 'look-see,' and that I was now free to leave this place and its haunting memories; that I didn't live in a house surrounded by bars, gates, and guards; and that I was free to walk the streets of Edinburgh unrecognized!

35

Greyfriars Bobby

"Moreover, the dogs came and licked his sores . . ."
—Luke 16:21

"Edinburgh's Royal Mile is the epitome of Old Edinburgh. Made up of four linked streets—Castlehill, Lawmarket, High Street, and Cannongate—the mile descends the sloping back of a long, steep-sided ridge from Edinburgh Castle at the west end to the Palace of Holyroodhouse at the east end. On either side of the Royal Mile are tall buildings, riddled with courtyards and passageways known as 'closes' and separated by narrow streets known as 'wynds.' All the way down the Royal Mile, historic buildings punctuate the general streetscape, and there are numerous stores, cafes, restaurants, and pubs. There are many things to see, including the Old Town Weaving Company, where tartan cloth is made; the Outlook Tower; Highland Tobooth, a handsome Gothic building with the tallest spire in Edinburgh; the Hub, Edinburgh's festival center; Gladstone's Land, a 17th century merchant's house; Lady Stair's house, where some of Scotland's finest writers, like Robert Burns, Robert Louis Stevenson, and Sir Walter Scott, are remembered . . ." and on and on went Sky, but the place that touched Coleen and me the most along the Royal Mile was a monument to a small dog!

Before coming to Scotland, I had heard of Edinburgh's most famous dog; I had even used the story of this dog in a sermon or two, but it wasn't until we passed the bronze statue of the terrier that the tale and legend came back. This Skye terrier's devotion to his dead master is forever enshrined in Edinburgh folklore. This is how the story goes:

"The famous Greyfriars Bobby was a trained police dog who worked with his master, Constable John Gray, guarding livestock at Edinburgh's city market, the Grassmarket, during the 1850s. When Gray died in 1858 at the age of 45, he was buried in Greyfriars churchyard, and his devoted terrier followed the remains of his beloved master to his gravesite. What began on that funeral day became a 14-year vigil by his master's grave. Bobby lingered near the grave until his own death nearly a decade and a half later. Over those years, the dog was cared for and beloved by everybody in the neighborhood. After the faithful companion's death, a statue of Greyfriars Bobby was placed at the junction of Candlemarker Row and the George IV Bridge."

As we drove past the exceptional dog's memorial, I thought of Lazarus's dogs and how Luke memorialized them in Jesus' story of the famous rich man and Lazarus. I have found it true that God's creatures sometimes show greater virtues than God's crowning creation: man. The loyalty, devotion, and faithfulness of Greyfriars Bobby are stinging rebukes to most of us. The vigil he kept and the perseverance he showed over those 14 years is beyond description. The trip down the Royal Mile was not only enlightening, but also inspiring: all because of the memory of a small dog!

36

Shopping on Princes Street

"Seek, and ye shall find..."
—Matthew 7:7

AROUND NOON on October 29th, Coleen and I were dropped off in front of the Hard Rock Café of Edinburgh with the rest of our traveling companions for an afternoon of shopping along Edinburgh's famous shopping district: Princes Street. We had actually been dropped off on Georges Street, which parallels Princes Street. I was on the lookout for some Scottish fishing flies, and Coleen was looking for Scottish sweaters. Eon had told me of an Orvis Fishing Shop at the end of Georges Street, so we started our shopping by walking the length of the famous street. It was a cool afternoon, but the walk warmed us up nicely.

After walking about 15 minutes, we discovered the Orvis Shop right where Eon said it would be. I bought five trout flies and five salmon flies, and according to the shop attendant, they were the most-used flies in Scotland for those two species of fish. I was sad to learn, however, that the beautiful flies were not made in Scotland but Kenya! I would have to be content with buying them in Scotland.

Shopping on Princes Street 75

After paying a few pounds and pence for the prize flies, Coleen and I turned the corner onto Princes Street.

The first place we stopped was what would become Coleen's favorite Scottish store: the Edinburgh Woolen Shop. We were hoping they would have a better price on sweaters than the store we found in Broadway, but they did not; if anything, they were more expensive. It wasn't a waste however because it was there I found the object of my second quest: a hat with Edinburgh, Scotland, on it. Ever since I went to Paris, France, to pick up my daughter Marnie and got a Paris hat, I have wanted an Edinburgh hat. (A sad footnote . . . I would lose this special hat on another foreign adventure when on a beach in Southern India I accidentally left it behind after a walk through the surf on Eve's Beach.) Moving down the street, we eventually came to a very fancy store called 'Romanes and Paterson,' and it was here that Coleen found what she was looking for.

Besides herself, Coleen had been looking for sweaters for her boss and his wife. The old shop, established in 1808, was a gold mine for such things. As Coleen looked for the right size and color, I looked around the rest of the store. It was here that I found the tape by Roger Whittaker that contained our trip's theme song, "All of My Life." Returning to Coleen, I found her with an arm full of Scottish sweaters and a few other treasures. We paid the bill and walked out of 'Romanes and Paterson' looking like tourists with our hands full of bags. We walked the length of Princes Street and did pick up a few postcards on the way, but we had found what we were looking for. The items on our 'wish lists' from Edinburgh were all checked off.

Isn't it wonderful when you 'seek and find?' Not only had our Lord brought us to this wonderful land, but He gave us the desires of our hearts in that wonderful land! Small items that will forever remind us that no matter homeland or foreign land, if you seek, you will find, even if what you are looking for is the old spark of love that starts your love-fire burning all over again!

37

A Scottish Hot Dog Under Scott's Monument

*". . . For every creature of God is good, and nothing to be
refused, if it be received with thanksgiving."*
—I Timothy 4:4

MY WIFE and I finished our shopping stroll along Princes Street by stopping for a bit to eat at a new mall just across the street from Sir Walter Scott Park. You can imagine my surprise when I discovered you could buy hot dogs—my favorite meat—in Scotland. After I got my foot-long hot dog, and Coleen bought a McDonald's hamburger meal, we decided to take advantage of the lovely afternoon and eat our American food in the park!

Under the shadow of a huge granite monument to the famous Scotsman, we ate lunch. Edinburgh's favorite son was inflicted with a childhood illness that left him lame in one leg. While his father was an Edinburgh lawyer, Scott spent most of his boyhood at his grandfather's farm in the country. It was there he learned to love storytelling and reading. He grew out of his lameness, studied law, and started a practice with his father. His job took him to the Highlands of Scotland, and he soon fell in love with the wild, rugged country. It was through these experiences and the stories of his aunt, mother, and old friends that he began to write poems and novels. His most famous poem is "The Lady of the Lake," and his most well-known novel is *Ivanhoe*, both still very popular even today. And here I was sitting under the statue of one of the world's great poets and storytellers!

I enjoyed the last rays of a late afternoon Scotland sun as I ate my first Scottish hot dog. The busy city traffic couldn't diminish the joy of the place and the memories of the man whose name adorned the gardens my wife and I were sitting in. My wife and I sat side-by-side on a park bench and enjoyed the flavor and savor of our Edinburgh lunch. The sun was dropping behind the high shops on Princes Street when we finished, and the evening chill was returning with the dying light. As my wife put on my head my new Edinburgh cap, and we headed across the street to our waiting bus on Georges Street, I thought of this line from *Ivanhoe*:

"She placed upon the drooping head of the victor the splendid chaplet which was the destined reward of the day."

It took Coleen and me about 15 minutes to find our way back to the Cosmo bus. We had gotten confused in our travels, so we made a couple wrong turns, but once we got our bearings we were not long finding our way. As I boarded the bus, I thanked Eon for his help in finding the 'flies' I was looking for. Once I got to my seat, I offered up a prayer of thanksgiving for the marvelous day the Lord had given my wife and me in Edinburgh. It had been filled with unexpected blessings and wonderful sites. I had a chance to not only experience a taste of Scotland (the hot dog was great), but also to taste firsthand the history of the land I for so long had only read about in Scott's books and poems!

38

Britannia

". . . that there was none other boat there . . ."
—John 6:22

ANOTHER SPECIAL treat during our only full day in Edinburgh was an unexpected trip to see the Royal Yacht Britannia at the Ocean Terminal in Leith, Scotland. Because some parts of the trip had been taken off the tour due to the lateness of the season, Roseann and Eon decided to add this special showing of the old royal yacht to our evening schedule before having supper at Edinburgh's most elegant restaurant.

From 1953 to 1997, the Royal Yacht Britannia served the royal family of England, traveling over a million miles to become one of the most famous ships in the world. Sailing to every corner of the globe in its career, the Britannia's voyages covered 968 royal and official visits. The yacht served Her Majesty the Queen and the Royal Family as a royal residence and for official government receptions, glittering state visits, royal honeymoons, and relaxing family holidays. Interestingly, when the yacht was retired in 1997, the Scottish government bought it and turned it into a tourist attraction, literally building a mall around it. We had to go through a department store to get to it!

Our tour started on the royal bridge just as the sun was setting behind the Firth of Forth Bridge in the far distance. Instead of having a personal tour guide, we were given individual hand-held recorders that we could program to tell us what we were seeing in each section of the ship. From the top deck, Coleen and I worked our way along the side of the ship until we got to the back deck. It was there we had our picture taken by the ship's bell. From there we worked our way down to the second deck, where we saw the Sun Lounge. I was surprised after the palaces we had seen to find the ship quite simple. On the third deck, we walked through the state dining room and the royal bedrooms; the king and queen had separate bedrooms!

We eventually worked our way through the five decks, seeing everything from the engine room to the laundry room to the wardroom and the chief petty officer's mess. Next to the dock was the royal boat that took the royal family from the yacht to land. Throughout the ship, the walls were covered with pictures of the royal family and the Britannia in just about every harbor around the world. The collection of photographs was highlighted with exhibitions of royal artifacts in most every area of the boat where there was an empty space. It took Coleen and I about an hour and a half to finish the tour, ending up in (of course) the gift shop, where you could buy almost anything connected with the Royal Yacht. Coleen and I bought a few postcards for our second honeymoon scrapbook—another page for our love story.

I found it ironic that the symbol of English sea power was now docked in a Scottish firth, making money for the Scots and not the Brits!

39

Great Supper at the George

"A certain man made a great supper..."
—Luke 14:16

COLEEN AND I thought we had arrived when we had supper at the Savoy-Simpson-in-the-Strand in London, but that world famous restaurant is nothing in comparison with The George in Edinburgh. I can say without a shadow of a doubt that the most elegant and charming restaurant I have ever eaten at in my life is The George!

Our travels took us back into downtown Edinburgh after our tour of the Britannia. We had seen the outside of The George restaurant on our afternoon shopping spree, but the outside looked just like the other buildings in the area—grey granite. It isn't until you step into The George that you understand the motto of the restaurant: "Sometimes a seat by the window is not a priority."

Built over 200 years ago by Robert Adam, the interior was nothing short of royal. I couldn't imagine that the Queen of England had a fancier dining room in any of her palaces. The huge room has a massive glass dome in the middle of the ceiling, and the roof is held up with twenty-foot marble pillars. The room is lit in the daytime with natural light from the dome and ceiling-to-floor windows in the back of the main room, but at night, the main light source is from golden chandeliers on both sides of the room. The light is soft and low and very romantic. My wife would tell you that it is the most romantic restaurant she has ever been in. There are tables for eating lined up behind the giant pillars, but we were ushered in and asked to sit on the main floor in cozy booths. There was a feast set for a king on just the first course table! We had come for a three-course meal, and it was like nothing I had ever eaten before.

I am a 'meat and potatoes' lover, and on that night at The George I samples three kinds of meat: wonderful roast lamb, mouth-watering roast turkey, and superb roast beef. We ate to our hearts' content. The dessert table was just as full with a variety of sweets, as was the salad bar. I was not only full when I finished; I knew that I had probably just eaten the greatest meal of the trip, and maybe my lifetime. I can say with confidence that the only feast that will beat that supper in Scotland will be my first meal in Heaven, or just perhaps, Bob Cote's famous steak and lobster lunch!

The meal was topped off with a bus ride back through the city to see Edinburgh Castle in lights. We traveled again through Princes Street to view the fabled capitol at night. The light show only added to the heavenly night Coleen and I had at The George. We got back to the Greens Motel around 8:30 p.m. We spent the last few hours of the day repacking for our trip out of Scotland the next day. Both Coleen and I agreed that night: if the Good Lord allows it, we will be back in the country and city that had captured our hearts! (We are still waiting and planning a 40th anniversary trip to the fabled land of Scotland.)

40

Jedburgh Jewelry

"In that day, when I make up my jewels..."
—Malachi 3:17

When Coleen and I awoke on October 30, 2003, our beloved Edinburgh was covered in fog, and a light rain was falling. If we had come to Scotland a day later, our wonderful day in the Scottish capitol would have been a washout—our Father's timing is perfect. The perfect panoramic view from our hotel was gone, but not from our minds. It was a bittersweet morning as we finished our last meal in Scotland and boarded the bus for England, but we already knew we would be stopping in Scotland two more times before we actually left our new favorite country.

As only the Lord can do, the farther Edinburgh was behind us, the clearer the weather became. And by the time we got to Jedburgh, Scotland, the sun was out and we had no use for our still-unused umbrella. We had stopped in Jedburgh for two reasons: it was our last chance to pick up anything Scottish we had missed in Edinburgh, and to visit Jedburgh Abbey. We went shopping first. It was in Jedburgh that Coleen got the last item on her United Kingdom wish list. My dear wife loves jewelry, and she was hoping to find some special jewelry on the trip to remember it by. She didn't know exactly what she was looking for, but in Jedburgh she found it: heather jewelry—fine jewelry, like earrings, pins, and necklaces, made from Scottish heather right off the moors. The colors were beautiful, and before she was through, she had three pieces, one of which was made in the shape of the spear thistle, Scotland's national flower! (Interestingly, Coleen bought this jewelry on the 20th anniversary of the salvation of our children, our dearest jewels!)

Our second stop in Jedburgh was at one of the most picturesque sites, in my opinion, on the whole tour. This is what I learned about Jedburgh Abbey:

"The abbey—its grand design inspired by Europe's magnificent churches—was founded in 1138 by David I. For the abbey's community of Augustinian canons, its location frequently landed them amidst conflict. When Anglo-Scottish relations deteriorated after 1296, Jedburgh became a front line target for English armies. The Reformation heralded the abbey's final decline. Despite this, it was used as the local church up to 1875, after which it became abandoned. Yet Jedburgh Abbey's remarkably complete Romanesque and early Gothic buildings have a tranquil stillness which belies their turbulent history."

I too found the ruined abbey a very peaceful place, nestled along the River Tweed. Of all the pictures I took in the UK, the one I chose to put by my computer as a remembrance was the one taken of Coleen and me with Jedburgh Abbey in the background: a picture of two lovers standing before the eternal outline of an ancient church. The events also reminded me of the message in an old church hymn, When He Cometh, by W. O. Cushing:

"When He cometh, when He cometh, to make up His jewels, all His jewels, precious jewels, His loved and His own. Like the stars of the morning, His bright crown adorning, they shall shine in their beauty bright gems for His crowns."

Like two pieces of heather jewelry called Barry and Coleen!

41

Standing Stones on the Scottish Border

"And these stones shall be for a memorial..."
—*Joshua 4:7*

Our last stop in Scotland was only fitting. We stopped on the border of Scotland and England for personal pictures by the two huge standing stones that mark the border—England is carved on one side, and Scotland carved on the other. I also took some great pictures of the heather on the hillsides and the bracken in full fall colors in the vale.

This stop was fitting when you take into account the bloody history between these two proud peoples. Never has history seen so many refugees as in the ancient history of the borderland between Scotland and England. All over the region, on both sides of the border, Roseann told story after story of the raids and counter-raids across this border. Uncounted multitudes had to leave home and country for safety elsewhere. As one reads their history, one's heart can't help but go out to frightened parents and hungry children trampling highway and byway, loaded and overloaded with all they could carry, bound for a refuge somewhere either north or south, victims of war. Though these standing stones were only placed on the border in recent times, the land they rest on could tell of countless crossings. Ours was a memorial crossing—and a meaningful one—as we took time to have our picture taken on both sides of the border.

As I walked to the brow of the hill to get my last pictures of Scotland, the sun had returned to us after the dense fog of Edinburgh. I had removed my coat and hat at Jedburgh to enjoy the warming air. The climate had changed, but the beauty of the land hadn't. The deep valleys and broad hillsides spoke only of the Lowlands of Scotland. There wasn't much of a change in terrain or territory as we moved from the Scottish Lowlands into the Northumberland National Park of England. To witness the peacefulness of the area, one would wonder why this land was so angrily fought over. I know from reading history, it was because of the constantly changing times and religious order, as well as the greed and hatred among men. As I walked back to the bus, I was reminded of something a favorite author, Vance Havner, once wrote:

"Let us remember that we are not thermometers to register the prevailing temperature but the thermostats to change it!"

If the Scots and English would have had a few more thermostats instead of a whole lot of thermometers, their border might have experienced warmer times. The last memorable event that took place on the border was the chance to see heather in full bloom. Roseann had put some in a pot on her last trip north, and Eon had kept it watered under the bus. I could only imagine what the entire region must have looked like when the light red heather filled the hills and valleys of the borderland! To this day, another dream of my dear Coleen is to return to this region when the heather is in full bloom and to dance together in the heather!

42

Laughing All the Way to York

"But he that is of a merry heart hath a continual feast."
—*Proverbs 15:15*

UPON LEAVING the Scottish/English border, Eon drove us through the Cheviot Hills and on to the wild region known as Northumberland National Park. Our destination was York, three hours away. On the most desolate part of our journey, we were entertained by Roseann, who was a very funny lady!

I don't know if the trip was just getting to her or not—we had been on the road for nearly a week now—but the tales Roseann told brought laughter to everyone on the bus. As we neared Newcastle, Eon's hometown, Roseann began to tell of the 'Angel of the North,' a modern piece of art that was known far and wide as the worst piece of art in the nation. Apparently, the artist had convinced the local population to invest in his 'masterpiece.' But before we arrived at the hill where the 'angel' was standing, we stopped for lunch at a 'moto'—a truck stop. This was an adventure we had yet to experience in this country.

Coleen and I shared a sandwich, a bag of chips, and a candy bar. While we watched people come in and out, we joked with our traveling companions. We especially got a big kick out of our new friends from the Philippines. They were delightful young people, full of fun. Eric was especially funny telling of the hotels and motels he has stayed in on his many trips to far off places. He, like Roseann, kept us entertained as we journeyed on.

Getting back on the bus, our first stop wasn't the infamous 'angel' but, just for me! Eon took us by a piece of Hadrian's Wall, located on a residential street in Newcastle. Hadrian was one of the most able of the Roman emperors, having been trained by the great soldier-emperor, Trajan. While he was emperor, Hadrian brought the empire of Rome to its greatest heights, which included the British Isles. To protect the borders of Britain from the northern barbarians, he built a wall across the entire width of the island, over 76 miles. Large sections of the wall can still be seen today, nearly 1,900 years after its construction. I was the only one that got off the bus to have my picture taken beside the section in Newcastle. It was another one of the special treats I didn't expect to experience on the tour. My heart was filled with a merry feast!

The final laugh on this section of the trip took place as we drove by the so-called 'Angel of the North.' It was the laughingstock of the country because it was indeed the poorest representation of an angel I have ever seen. The entire bus had a good laugh as we sailed by the structure. We didn't even stop to see it up close and personal; 1,900-year-old stones were more meaningful and memorable to me.

43

What's in a Word?

"Then said they unto him, say now Shibboleth: and he said Sibboleth: for he could not frame to pronounce it right. Then they took him, and slew him at the passages..."
—Judges 12:6

ANOTHER THING Coleen and I did on our long ride from Scotland to York, England's most medieval city was make a list of the strange English words we had come across, or the strange meanings the English had given to certain words we were familiar with. These are the English words we found interesting:

A soda pop was called 'soft.'
A circle was called a 'circus.'
A diaper was called a 'nappy.'
A bus was called a 'coach.'
A pacifier was called a 'dummy.'
An RV or motor home was called a 'caravan.'
A highway was called a 'motorway.'
A bar was called a 'pub.'
A yield sign was called a 'give way.'
An elevator was called a 'lift.'

A subway was called an 'underground.'
A bathroom was called a 'toilet.'
A line was called a 'queue.'
A vacation was called a 'holiday.'
Sneakers were called 'trainers.'
Gas was called 'petrol.'
A taxi was called a 'cab.'
A policeman was called a 'bobby.'
French fries were called 'chips.'
Cream was called 'crème.'
Potato chips were called 'crisps.'
Ham was called 'bacon.'
A bay was called a 'firth.'

Coleen and I had very few problems with the language for the most part, with the exception of the night I tried to explain to a ticket agent in London where I wanted to go. Because I wanted to go one way, and she wanted to direct me another way, I raised my voice to get my point across. She immediately questioned, "Sir, are you attacking me?" At first I didn't understand what she meant by 'attacking,' seeing as there was a wall of two-inch bulletproof glass between us. She took the tone of my voice as an assault. All I could think of was the time when the men of Ephraim were able to determine who the Gileadites were because they couldn't form the 'sh' sound in Shibboleth. I was glad the punishment for a raised question wasn't the same as with the Gileadites.

Overall, Coleen and I enjoyed the British, Welsh, and Scottish accents we heard. Even on occasion, a few people were taken by our Maine brogue!

44

Strolling through the Shambles

"Walk about Zion, and go round about her:
tell the towers thereof."
—Psalms 48:12

WE DROVE into York, England, around two o'clock on the afternoon of October 30th. We had the rest of the day to explore two thousand years of English history, overshadowed by Britain's largest medieval cathedral: York Minster.

Roseann took us on a walking tour of this ancient city by first guiding us through the old city walls to the front of the magnificent cathedral. York Cathedral's present foundations were laid by the Normans in the 12th century. The massive walls of the church are crowded with dramatic monuments, as are the surrounding grounds, including a statue of Constantine, the only emperor of Rome crowned in Britain. The central tower soars over 200 feet above the town, and the great East window is as big as a tennis court, the largest medieval stained glass window in the world. Coleen and I had a chance to walk completely around this superb building, and we were impressed.

Strolling through the Shambles

Before cutting us free, Roseann walked us down to the famous 'shambles' of York. One of the appeals of York is largely due to the survival of its central streets in their original form. While other cities we visited had been remodeled over the years, York had been spared any wholesale change. Many of the buildings in the 'shambles' are original, not restored or rebuilt. As we walked down through Stonegate, we followed the exact line of the Roman approach road of 71 AD. Narrow cobblestone streets were overhung by timber-framed houses. There was one street in which the houses had bent over the street as a tree would over a shady lane. Eventually, the narrow lane, full of people when we were there, led us to Newgate Market. It was from here Coleen and I bought a couple of homemade doughnuts from a street vendor—they were marvelously tasty!

The maze of quaint streets also led us to an open market where just about anything could be purchased. It was the most people we had seen on the streets of England. It was a sunny day, and once again the Lord had given us perfect weather to walk about. We also found a place to exchange the last of our money: 85 pounds and 65 pence for $150 US. It was then Coleen decided she needed a cup of tea, but the only place we could find one was at a Starbucks! Getting it to go, Coleen and I did a lot of window shopping as we headed back toward the Ouse River Bridge and our bus. The afternoon was quickly fading, and we still had an hour and a half ride before we reached our motel in Rotherham. Before we got on the bus, however, I left Coleen in a small park to finish her tea while I took a walk along the old city wall in search of a camera angle to take a panoramic picture of the city with the cathedral in the background. My last walk in York was successful, towers and all!

45

Rain in Rotherham

"And his favour is as a cloud of the latter rain . . ."
—*Proverbs 16:15*

It took us nearly an hour and a half to travel from York to our motel in Rotherham, Yorkshire, England. We would spend our last night away from London at the Marriott Courtyard Hotel on West Bawtry Road, the most modern motel we stayed at during the entire trip.

After settling into our very nice room—the bed had a duvet on it just like in London—we went downstairs and had a wonderful three-course meal in the motel restaurant. I had the pork—not as good as the Olive Garden at home, but very tasty indeed. Returning to our room, Coleen and I spent the rest of the evening relaxing and reminiscing over the things we had seen and experienced. That night we compiled a couple of lists; first was a list of all the animals we had seen on our trips through the English countryside:

1. Many kinds of sheep
2. Many kinds of beef cattle
3. Pigs
4. Chickens
5. Lots of Canadian geese

6. Swans
7. Pheasant
8. Llamas
9. Many kinds of birds
10. Rabbits
11. Holsteins
12. Dogs, but few cats! (We were getting homesick for our cat, Precious Pearl.)

Second was a list of the weather we'd had:

Oct. 23—Cloudy with snow squalls in Maine, 40s

Oct. 24—Overcast with some sun in London, 50s

Oct. 25—Sunny to cloudy with showers in the evening, 50s

Oct. 26—Frost to start, then sunny, and later broken clouds, 50s

Oct. 27—Mostly sunny all day, 60s

Oct. 28—Overcast, then showers, and rain in the evening, 50s

Oct. 29—Broken clouds, then sunny, 60s

Oct. 30—Heavy fog, then broken clouds, and later showers, 50s

(We still hadn't used our umbrella!)

We went to sleep around 10:30 p.m. and had a wonderful night's rest. When we awoke on our last full day in the United Kingdom, it was raining in Rotherham. It was the hardest rain we had seen, but once again we were on the road. After our last full English breakfast, we boarded the bus for the Midlands of England and the small town of Stamford in Lincolnshire. For the next two hours, we passed though some of the richest farmlands in Britain. On the way, we went by Thirsk, where some of my favorite English gentlemen lived in the town of Darrowby. I am of course speaking of *All Creatures Great and Small* and of James Herriot, Siefried, and Tristen. We also traveled through the famous Sherwood Forest just outside of Nottingham, and as we neared Stamford, the rain let up! It was as if the 'Eternal Weatherman' was clearing the way each and every time we needed to walk outside!

46

Window Shopping in Stamford

*"Then I saw, and considered it well:
I looked upon it, and received instruction."*
—*Proverbs 24:32*

SURE ENOUGH, the minute we drove into Stamford, it stopped raining. The clouds remained, but as we walked into town from the bus stop, the air was clear of precipitation. Coleen and I could tell from the start we would like Stamford. It was bigger than Broadway but had the same characteristics. Just to get into town we took the water route along the Welland River. By now you know of my love of water, especially rivers and streams, brooks and creeks. The River Welland flowed along the edge of town in an area known as the meadows. A small walking bridge crossed the river into a large open field that ran the entire length of the town. On the bridge, I took a beautiful picture of an English lassie (young lady) feeding the local duck family.

Our next stop, for we had less than an hour to explore this typical English town, was Barn Hill and the many shops along the cobblestone streets. We window shopped until we came to a kitchen store. My wife was still planning her Christmas Tea for 2003, and she was on the lookout for some special items. She had gotten her tea for the Tea in London, but it was in Stamford that she purchased the rest, including tea spoons, a tea apron, and an assortment of other tea-related items. By a little after ten o'clock, we were back on the bus, and you guessed it: it was raining again, and our umbrella still hadn't gotten wet!

As I had since we began our English tour, I started my stop watch, and I added it to this list:
Heathrow to London—43 minutes
London to Hampton—38 minutes
Hampton to Salisbury—93 minutes
Salisbury to Stonehenge—32 minutes
Stonehenge to Bath—105 minutes
Bath to Cardiff—126 minutes
Cardiff to Tintern—26 minutes
Tintern to Broadway—98 minutes
Broadway to Stratford—33 minutes
Stratford to Llangollen—122 minutes
Llangollen to Wrexham—37 minutes
Wrexham to Chester—35 minutes
Chester to Grasmere—126 minutes
Grasmere to Gretna Green—68 minutes
Gretna Green to Edinburgh—156 minutes
Edinburgh to Jedburgh—89 minutes
Jedburgh to Newcastle—95 minutes
Newcastle to York—89 minutes
York to Rotherham—91 minutes
Rotherham to Stamford—103 minutes
Stamford to Cambridge—48 minutes

And every one of those minutes I was sitting beside the love of my life, and doing a lot of window watching. Rather window shopping or window watching, England, Scotland, and Wales were some of the best times I had experienced in my life. What a joy!

47

And I, Even I Only, Am Left

". . . and I, even I only, am left . . ."
—I Kings 19:14

WE ROLLED into the famous university town of Cambridge around eleven o'clock on October 31, 2003. This would be our last stop on the tour until we arrived back in London. As she had done so many times before, Roseann took us on a walking tour of the town before setting us loose to shop or sightsee or stroll. Because there are 32 colleges in the Cambridge University system, she highlighted the others by zeroing in on one, Queen's College. Actually, she took us for a walk around the massive campus. We saw the world-famous chapel, peaked into one of the inner courtyards, and got up close and personal with some of the students on their bikes. Because of the narrow streets and the multitude of students, no cars are allowed in the center of town. Bikes are the favored method of transportation in Cambridge. Once we had a general idea of the layout of the center of Cambridge, we were off to the city market. Coleen had one more item to purchase—a piece of cloth.

We wandered awhile looking for King's College, but soon discovered it was too far away to justify the walk.

And I, Even I Only, Am Left   101

Returning to the city center, we soon found the local market and within a short time, Coleen was talking to a man about a piece of cloth. My wife loves to quilt, and she was looking for a special piece of English cloth that she could use in a quilt pattern she was developing. As she looked, I wandered around the square taking pictures of the massive college buildings and the activities of a typical English market. It was then I heard his deep, booming voice.

Just before me was a street preacher proclaiming the Good News of Jesus Christ! He was an older man, probably in his 60s, with a powerful voice. He was tall and gray-headed, dressed as everyone else. He was wearing a light coat to keep warm in the damp air, but his tone was clear and urgent as he preached to the shoppers and students in the square. I was drawn to him and his message because I too had stood as a young college student on the street corners of Greenville, South Carolina, and preached to passing strangers. It wasn't long, however, before I realized that of all the people in the square—and there were hundreds—I was the only individual listening to this aging evangelist. Nobody was stopping what they were doing to listen to him, and they walked by him as if he was just another one of the many statues lining the square. I said a short prayer for the unknown preacher as he warned those passing by of the coming judgment. I left him preaching, exhorting, and telling, but as I walked away, I thought of Elijah and how he felt when he complained to the Lord, "And I, even I only, am left!" Each generation will face a time when apathy abounds, and the lone voice of the evangelist is heard in the street and nobody, but nobody, is listening except another preacher just passing through!

48

Crossing the Cam in Cambridge

"Neither shouldest thou have stood in the crossway..."
—Obadiah 14

Returning to find my wife still looking over fabric, I wandered to the other side of the square. It was there I found another 'to-do' item on our British goals list: having lunch at a typical English tea shop. Once Coleen found the right piece of cloth for her memory quilt, I invited her to lunch at Auntie's Tea Shop. The small tea store and restaurant was tucked away in a side alley near Queen's College. The tables in the front of the store were all full, so we found a table for two near the door in the back of the shop. The back room was as crowded as the front, but the atmosphere was still very British. I looked at my watch as we began to eat our meal, knowing our time was getting short. We were due on the bus by one o'clock—we had just enough time for tea!

Our meal was a typical English sandwich and English tea with an English cookie on the side. I knew when we finished our lunch that Auntie's Tea Shop would have to go on my Top Ten Special Places We Ate in the United Kingdom list:

1. British Airway's Executive Lounge, Boston
2. The Savoy: Simpson's on the Strand, London
3. Two Bridges Pub, Edinburgh
4. The George, Edinburgh
5. Harrods's Café, London
6. Fish and Chips on the banks of the Thames River
7. Salisbury Café at Salisbury Cathedral
8. On the canal at Stratford-upon-Avon
9. Walter Scott Park, Edinburgh
10. Auntie's Tea Shop, Cambridge

Just as we finished our lunch, a British military man came up to us and volunteered to take our picture. It was a nice touch to an already special experience. As we walked back to the bus across the Cam River, I had one more joyous trick to play on my wife. Throughout the entire tour, I had always fallen behind my wife because I was snapping last-minute photographs. Our walk, if not a jaunt, out of Cambridge took us across the River Cam Bridge (the 'cam' in 'Cambridge,' and there is also a 'bridge' in Cambridge!). Once again I got caught trying to take one last picture of the beautiful riverside on the bridge over the Cam River. By the time I was through, my wife was a good hundred yards in front of me. She yelled back that I was going to be late for the bus, to which I shouted that I would still beat her to the bus. As she pressed on up the walkway, I cut across the park so that by the time she turned the corner, I was standing by a lamppost asking her what took her so long. I will never forget the smile on her face as we joked our way back to the bus. It was just one of the fun things I will always remember from this very, very fun trip!

49

The Cambridge Seven

*"And I heard the voice of the Lord, saying,
Whom shall I sent, and who will go for us?"*
—Isaiah 6:8

As I boarded the bus for London, my heart and mind were still in Cambridge. One of the reasons I was happy that our British Isles tour had stopped in Cambridge was so I could tread the 'holy ground' once walked by the famous 'Cambridge Seven.'

England, Scotland, and Wales have produced some of the greatest heroes of the Christian Church—men like 'Christmas' Evans of Wales, David Livingstone of Scotland, and William Carey of England. One of my favorite from the British Isles was a fellow by the name of C.T. Studd. Born into a wealthy family, Charles Studd was sent to Cambridge University by his father, Edward, for the best education money could buy. But before he was through, Studd would be known as the premier cricketer in all of England. As captain of the Cambridge Cricket Team, Studd became a name known far and wide. Despite the fact that he had been converted in 1876 at the age of 16, it wasn't until 1884 that he gave his whole being to Christ, and he did it at the height of his fame as a sports hero.

In 1884, C.T. (as he was best known) went to a farewell service conducted by a little-known mission that had just started up 19 years before—the China Inland Mission, directed by Hudson Taylor. After that meeting, Studd knew that God was leading him to China and that he was to give up all desire to work in government and become a missionary instead. He, like Isaiah before him, had heard God's question. Studd's decision to sacrifice an easy life at home for the hardships of missionary life in distant China started a revival on the university campus at Cambridge. With Studd went S.P. Smith, the man who had taken Studd to the meeting (he was a close friend of Studd) and a great oarsman for the Cambridge rowing team; and M. Beauchcamp, A.T. Polhill-Turner, D.E. Hoste, C.H. Polhill-Turner, and W.W. Cassels. In their farewell meeting on February 5, 1885, the campus at Cambridge and the entire country were buzzing with the progress of the 'Cambridge Band,' later known as 'The Cambridge Seven.' Each was from a well-to-do family, yet they gave up fame and fortune to serve Christ in China. Their testimonies stirred many others from English universities to go into overseas mission.

As Eon drove us out of Cambridge and onto the M1 toward London, I thought how Britain had become a nation of onlookers, a grandstand generation—watching the play but never getting into the action. I saw no sign of 'The Cambridge Seven' in Cambridge, just a population of professional spectators. Everything left in Cambridge was geared to showmanship and entertainment that involved no commitment. C.T. Studd and his friends would be quite sad, as I was. My fear is that America is following its native land even in this example of being a fan instead of a player!

50

Last Night in London

"Also day by day, from the first day unto the last day..."
—Nehemiah 8:18

WE ARRIVED back at the Thistle Motel at Euston, just outside London, in the middle of the afternoon on October 31st. We repacked our luggage for the trip home on the morrow, and then headed to Euston Station for a subway ride back into London Town. We were going to have supper at the original Hard Rock Café.

My wife was a huge Beatles fan in the 60s, and she wanted to see some paraphernalia of the famous singing group in their native land. We took the London underground to Hyde Park but got turned around after we arrived at Green Station. We walked in the wrong direction for about a block before finally realizing something was wrong. We stopped to talk to the doorman at the Ritz—he was very nice and got us on the right track again. Crossing the street, we walked nearly 10 minutes with Hyde Park on our left before coming to the now worldwide restaurant chain. What was playing on the big-screen televisions was a clip from a documentary on the Beatles with them singing one of their more famous hits: "I Want to Hold Your Hand."

The café was packed with Halloween party goers (another memory we will never forget: spending Halloween in London), and the tables were all full except for one downstairs. We were ushered into the basement where we split a BLT, some onion rings, and a soda for $32.88! Rock and Roll is expensive! It was nice if the music wasn't loud, but the best part of the evening was the walk back to the subway and the ride to our motel by way of the underground. It was a cool evening, but the lights were bright and two honeymooners from Maine were enjoying each others company in one of the great cities of the world. (Can there be anything more romantic than strolling the streets of London Town with the most beautiful girl in the world on your arm?) The last day of our stay in London ended as well as our first day in London: together, exploring, and on an adventure.

When we got back to the Thistle, I made another list in my little red book (how I kept track of times, places, and other things to write stories and record memories)—Cities and Towns We Stopped In:

1. London, England
2. Salisbury, England
3. Bath, England
4. Cardiff, Wales
5. Broadway, England
6. Stratford, England
7. Llangollen, Wales
8. Wrexham, Wales
9. Chester, England
10. Grasmere, England
11. Gretna Green, Scotland
12. Edinburgh, Scotland

13. Jedburgh, Scotland
14. Newcastle, England
15. York, England
16. Rotherham, England
17. Stamford, England
18. Cambridge, England

And to think that I visited all these place with the dearest lady in the world; the very thing that makes these places and visits so special!

Postlude: Many Miracles

"Write the things which thou hast seen,
and the things which are . . ."
—Revelation 1:19

NOVEMBER 2003 arrived, and my wife and I had to head back to Maine from our second honeymoon in the British Isles. We took the same shuttle van back to Heathrow Airport with the same six ladies from Massachusetts we had arrived with. We also picked up five people from Cape Cod at another Thistle Motel; they were returning home from a 15-day tour of southern England. When we arrived at Heathrow, we discovered a terminal full of people. It took us an hour and a half just to get to the ticket counter. Once we got through the security check, Co and I spent our last pound and pence on water and Cadbury Chocolate—one of the special foods, along with shortbread cookies, that we brought back with us. And right on time, our plane was called and we were off across the Atlantic for another rendezvous with one of our Lord's great miracles on this trip!

On the way back across the 'pond,' I made my final lists, including Famous Rivers We Crossed:

1. The Thames, London

2. The Severn, Wales

3. The Wye, Wales

4. The Avon, Stratford

5. The Dee, Llangollen

6. The Clyde, Scotland

7. The Tweed, Jedburgh

8. The Ouse, York

9. The Welland, Stamford

10. The Cam, Cambridge

And also, the Miles We Traveled:

Ellsworth to Bangor: 25

Bangor to Boston: 269

Boston to London: 3,280

London to Cardiff: 191

Cardiff to Wrexham: 230

Wrexham to Edinburgh: 273

Edinburgh to Rotherham: 255

Rotherham to London: 193

London to Boston: 3,280

Boston to Bangor: 269

Bangor to Ellsworth: 25

Total Miles: 8,290

When we arrived in Boston, we got through customs without being asked any questions or having to open anything. Our travel schedule called for a four-hour wait in Boston for the bus to Bangor, but in the final miracle of the trip, the Lord worked it out so we made a connection to South Station and picked up the earlier bus. So, we arrived home at 7 p.m. instead of 11 p.m. (or 4 a.m. London time!). If there is a verse for our trip, it has to be the question of the chief priests and Pharisees when they said of Jesus:

"What do we? For this man doth many miracles!" (John 11:47).

It was a miracle trip with many miracles along the way. It fulfilled every dream I had to give my dear wife a second honeymoon in a romantic place where love abounds. We still speak of our carefree day in the British Isles and dream of another trip in 2113. If it happens I will follow the instructions the Good Lord gave to Jeremiah:

"Thus speaketh the Lord God of Israel, saying, Write thee all the words that I have spoken unto thee in a book!" (Jeremiah 30:2)

—Barry Blackstone
November 1, 2003

www.ingramcontent.com/pod-product-compliance
Lightning Source LLC
Chambersburg PA
CBHW070925160426
43193CB00011B/1583